JR CARVER...

W9-AJU-721

The place of houses

Charles Moore

Gerald Allen

Donlyn Lyndon

With Axonometric Drawings
by William Turnbull

The place of houses

Holt, Rinehart and Winston
NEW YORK

Copyright © 1974 by Charles Moore, Gerald Allen, Donlyn Lyndon. All rights reserved, including the right to reproduce this book or portions thereof in any form.

Published by Holt, Rinehart and Winston, 383 Madison Avenue, New York, New York 10017.

Published simultaneously in Canada by Holt, Rinehart and Winston of Canada, Limited.

Library of Congress Cataloging in Publication Data
Moore, Charles
The place of houses.
1. Architecture, Domestic. 2. Architecture and climate. 3. Architecture and society. I. Lyndon, Donlyn, joint author. II. Allen, Gerald, joint author. III. Title.
NA7125.M66   728.3   70-182776
ISBN Hardbound: 0-03-007726-5
ISBN Paperback: 0-03-052361-3

First Holt Paperback Edition—1979

Designer: Madelaine Caldiero
Printed in the United States of America

10   9   8   7   6   5   4   3   2   1

Illustration credits

The first figure in each pair refers to the page number; the second figure (in parentheses) refers to the illustration number.

Dorothy Alexander, 119 (11)

Gerald Allen, 20 (1-2), 21 (3-4, 6), 22 (7-8), 23 (9-11), 24 (13-14), 25 (15-18), 26 (19-20), 27 (21-22), 33 (1), 34 (4), 41 (19-20), 42 (22), 43 (23), 44 (25-26), 46 (27-29), 96 (29-30), 106 (48), 107 (49), 112 (3), 128 (5), 149 (1-3), 185 (11), 191 (6), 192 (7), 193 (9), 194 (10), 196 (13), 200 (18), 201 (19), 202 (20), 212 (7), 215 (12), 236 (12)

Archiv Prestel Verlag, Munich, 120 (12)

Morley Baer, 28 (23-26), 30 (27), 36 (6-7), 38 (11-13), 39 (14-15), 47 (30), 53 (7), 54 (8), 55 (9-10), 56 (12-14), 57 (15-16), 58 (18-19), 60 (21), 61 (22-23), 62 (24), 64 (29-30), 65 (31-33), 66 (34), 90 (20-22), 116 (8-10), 120 (13), 122 (14), 151 (5-6), 156 (13), 157 (14), 178 (3), 179 (5), 180 (6), 181 (7)

Louis M. S. Beal, 264 (4)

Biltmore House and Gardens, 111 (2)

Paul David Birnbaum, 51 (2)

Buckingham Palace, 97 (31)

Country Life, 85 (14)

Roy Flamm, 97 (32)

Alexandre Georges, 135 (17)

John T. Hill, 63 (26-28)

Cortland V. D. Hubbard, 134 (13-15)

Thomas Jefferson Memorial Foundation, 131 (8)

Balthazar Korab, 137 (21-22), 191 (5)

Rollin LaFrance, 211 (6)

Maynard Lyndon, 236 (11)

Bill Maris, 161 (19-20), 162 (21), 163 (22), 217 (13), 218 (15), 219 (16-17), 220 (18)

Norman McGrath, 110 (1)

Charles Moore, 40 (18), 103 (45), 131 (9-10), 195 (11-12), 246 (1), 251 (2), 264 (3), 272 (1)

Museum of Modern Art, 139 (24-25), 177 (2)

Frederick E. Paton, 227 (1)

Robert Perron, 222 (20), 223 (21), 228 (2)

Wade Perry, 2 (1), 5 (3-4), 6 (5-6), 7 (7), 8 (8-9), 9 (10-11), 10 (12, 14), 12 (15), 13 (16), 15 (17-19), 16 (20-21), 17 (22), 18 (23), 100 (41), 105 (47), 130 (6-7), 235 (10)

James Righter, 51 (1), 168 (29), 197 (15), 198 (16)

Louis Schwarz, courtesy of Historic Charleston Foundation, 113 (4)

Maurice Smith, 229 (3)

Trustees of Sir John Soane's Museum, 104 (46), 230 (4), 231 (6), 232 (7), 233 (8), 234 (9)

Sports Illustrated Photo by Marvin E. Newman © Time, Inc., 33 (2)

Ezra Stoller, 136 (18-19), 137 (20), 210 (2-4), 211 (5), 214 (9-10), 215 (11)

A. Youngmeister, 34 (3)

Contents

A note on the drawings
All axonometric drawings, floor plans,
elevations, and sections (but not site plans,
section perspectives, or diagrams) are
reproduced at the same scale—32 feet to
the inch.

The authors especially thank William Turnbull,
who drew the axonometrics, and William
Durkee, who made nearly all of the other
drawings. They are also grateful to T. W.
Kleinsasser, who supplied the documents from
which the drawings of Fonthill (Mercer's Castle)
on page 133 were made, and to Philippe Boudon,
whose research on Le Corbusier's housing at
Pessac and Lège, published in *Lived-in
Architecture* (Cambridge, 1972), provided the
basis for the drawings on pages 141-142.

Foreword

Good taste, we are told, is a singularly important factor in the design of a house. We are usually told this by someone who is assumed to possess it, and who generally makes a considerable point of the rest of the assumption: that there are people who don't have it, that that includes you, and that you will have to pay dearly to be suitably worked over. We submit that all of this is arrant nonsense. Our traditions are far less confining than the "tastemakers" would have us believe. Traditions have great power precisely because they present us with possibilities and guides that can support invention (Thou Shalt . . .), while good taste seeks to intimidate us with rules and limitations that stifle personal choice (Thou Shalt Not . . .).

The main premise of this book is that any one who cares enough can create a house of great worth—no anointment is required. *If you care enough* you just do it. You bind the goods and trappings of your life together with your dreams to make a place that is uniquely your own. In doing so you build a semblance of the world you know, adding it to the community that surrounds you.

This is not at all to minimize the importance of expertise, only to discredit its mysteries. Certainly, expertise does inform choice. If you care about snuff boxes, brass hinges, or Chippendale chairs, you will soon develop a capacity for distinguishing the real from the fake, the superior from the ordinary. You have no need to be told whether your taste is good or not. If you are moved by the light from a particular window, or by the shape of the opening, you will learn to note its dimensions and orientation and compare them with others. You become expert by caring and working, not by the receipt of any gift from on high.

In areas where you don't care enough to develop expertise, the chances are that other traditional limits will quite automatically assert themselves. If, for instance, chairs are your passion you already know which ones mean the most to you—antique Etruscan ones, maybe, or fine classic modern ones that please your eyes and your body, or incredibly ingenious ones that employ surprising principles of balance. If, on the other hand, chairs are not your passion, why fake it? You can buy extraordinarily comfortable ones made of canvas on a folding frame for under twenty dollars, and save your money and time for something you do care about.

This book is based on the assumption that your house is of great interest and importance to you. We discuss things we know about in order that you may augment your expertise and gain confidence in your own observations and experience as a suitable basis for creating a house that is your own. If our assumption is wrong, and you do not care all that much, we can be of no help. You should then find a suitable furnished apartment and forget it.

We started out to write a pattern book for houses, inspired by the nineteenth-century pattern books that described a set of houses for people to emulate. We began with the premise that houses built today are mostly careless and terrible, that they had been built well in the past, and that pattern books had helped make them so. Therefore, a new pattern book was called for, and we set about devising one. As we considered what a new pattern book might include and how it might be helpful, we realized that it was not so much the patterns themselves that mattered but the way in which they were useful in focusing energy. The crucial ingredient is concern, care for the way that a house is built and the shape that it gives to your life. Pattern books had helped in the past by setting out the range of decisions to be made, directing attention to the several aspects of the house deemed most critical: roof, floor-plan and window types, usually, and the general stylistic trappings of the whole. For the nineteenth century this may have been, and for some people still is, enough. But our experience as architects leads us to believe that houses can and should be more completely suited to the lives of their inhabitants and to the specific places where they are built. No simple or even complex set of house patterns, however ingenious and skillful, would do.

People who consciously attempt to extend their lives by caring for their house would not be served by a book that offered whole house patterns for the taking. Tract builders already do that, with dismaying results. They substitute stereotype for personality, relentlessly casting the house buyer into a minimal exchange with his surroundings. They offer the inhabitant little, and he asks less, till finally the buyer's interest in making a house the center of his own world is reduced to nothing. We are writing for those of you who still think it important to make a place of your own and who have the energy to struggle with the problems of making it, whether with your own hands, or with the aid of an architect and builder, or by renovating a place already built. Our task, now, is to clarify choices, to focus your energy so that it will not all be spent trying to find a way through the muddle of building decisions, but instead can be used to bring your own personal concerns to bear. We are certain by now that care, liberated by knowledge and confidence and invested in a house, is an investment returnable with interest. As with long-standing beliefs about bread cast on the waters, this confidence is an act of faith. We believe that the contents of this book sustain that faith and describe the decisions that would translate needs and dreams, even follies and pretensions, into patterns of choice about your house.

The first chapters of the book describe three towns we admire greatly, each quite different, yet each enjoying a very special quality of shared architectural purpose. We look closely at these to see how they came to be, what lessons they offer, and where they fail. All three places are American; Edgartown on Martha's Vineyard has a clarity that comes from three centuries of general agreement among the inhabitants about what a good town might be like, as they made their separate houses; Santa Barbara, California, has an eccentric specialness consciously established during one moment in time when the inhabitants agreed to invent a form for the town that would connect it with a synthetic, romantic past; and Sea Ranch on the northern California coast is the product of an agreement among developers and consultants about the nature of the site, an agreement contrived before any inhabitants were present.

These three places, together with some individual houses that we've designed, set the stage for the central part of the book, our attempt to delineate the three conceptual building blocks from which houses are made: rooms to live in, machines that serve life, and the inhabitants' dreams made manifest.

We detail the finite number of ways that rooms can be assembled, be related to machines, and fitted to the land. We also discuss, with examples, some of the nearly infinite number of ways in which rooms can be adjusted for the special interest of those who inhabit them. A checklist is then included to help reveal to you the patterns of living your house must accommodate and to set you on the path to organizing the place that your house may become.

So this is a pattern book after all, but not in the sense we had first imagined. This one describes patterns that help you think about houses; we are not trying to impose shapes. If we put any new limits on your search for a good house then we will have failed. But if we have managed to make your search easier, or even more interesting, we can count our purpose achieved.

Houses in several places

1. *Edgartown from the harbor*

Edgartown

Edgartown, on Martha's Vineyard off the Massachusetts coast, is an old and very elegant village that is a testament to the art of building well. (1) It is so pleasant, so memorable, so redolent of a sense of place that it rewards not only continuing visits but detailed examination.

In 1671 the town was named for the infant son of James, Duke of York. Although Prince Edgar had unfortunately died some weeks before, the town has borne his name through three centuries of modest growth and striking change. In the eighteenth century, Edgartown was a center of agriculture and maritime commerce. Later on, and more luxuriously, it became a whaling port second in importance only to Nantucket. Today, more luxuriously still, it is a busy vacation resort where the houses, streets, and harbor, remnants of an industrious mercantile past, provide blandishments for summer residents and tourists.

Visitors almost always come to Edgartown by way of Vineyard Haven, where the largest ferries land. They drive along a small, straight road through scrub growth and pine thickets and, in due course, through predictably bland modern outskirts with their filling stations and garages and nondescript houses. The road from Vineyard Haven is simply something to be traveled along to get somewhere. At a spot marked by a flagpole it becomes a place to be, Edgartown's Main Street. (2)

Facing the intersection where the flagpole stands is the Joshua Snow house, simply and, to our eyes, admirably built in 1838 according to the traditional pattern of most other houses in Edgartown and indeed in all of New England in the eighteenth and early nineteenth centuries. (3) A wooden box a story and a half high with a gable roof, it contains a set of rooms around an entrance hall on the ground floor and secondary rooms above. Two slender chimneys pierce the roof just in front of its peak and vent the fireplaces in the house. Except for their tidy black caps they are painted white, like the boards of the house itself. Almost all the distinguishing details on the outside — the chimney caps, the shutters, the scroll brackets supporting the canopy over the front door — perform or at least recall some specific, useful, as well as decorative service.

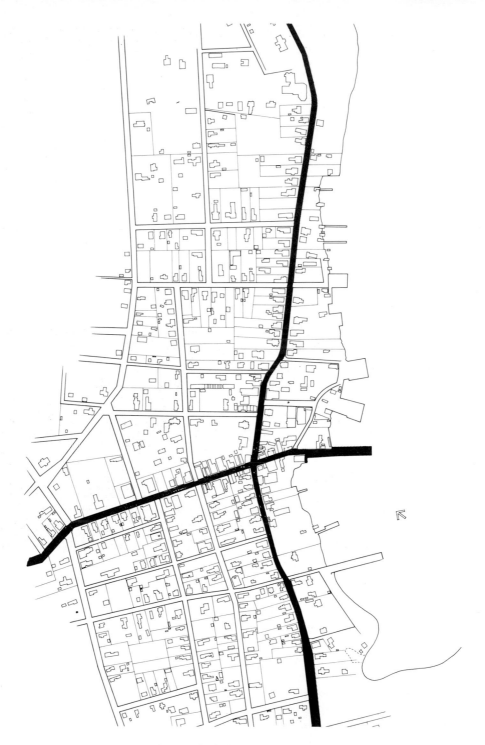

2. Plan of Edgartown, Main and Water Streets shaded

Even the white picket fence on either side of the front walk and along the sidewalk marks a boundary between the public realm and the private realm of the inhabitants.

The house is quite without overt attempts to be special, or even distinguishable from its neighbors. Edgartown in fact preserves the decorum of a black-tie dinner, where everyone manages to look his best while dressing very much like everyone else. Certain limited extravagances are allowed, like frills on a shirt or even a madras cummerbund, but there is a large area of agreement about forms, encouraged by an active and continuing tradition. There is pretty substantial agreement, too, about what cannot be included: no bare feet, or even clip-on ties or their residential equivalent: shutters nailed to the wall. Nothing in the Snow house is out of place; nothing is there without some point or conviction, some need, actual or remembered, and the house, because of all this good sense, speaks with a particularly strong voice.

Two doors down Main Street is the Daniel Fisher house, which speaks in rather different terms. (4) Dr. Fisher was a founder and first president of the Martha's Vineyard National Bank, and when he built his house he made it out of seasoned Maine pine fastened together entirely with brass and copper nails. With its carefully carved doorway and porch, the massive wood pilasters accenting each corner of the house, and the heavy cornice under the balustrade at the edge of the roof, it is much more elaborate than the Joshua Snow house up the street. Yet it, too, is simply a box which encloses a set of rooms around a central hall. Reproduced in New England timber, it takes much of its inspiration from the great stone houses of England, the villas of sixteenth-century Italy, or even the details of the architecture of Greece and Rome.

3. *Snow house, 1838*

4. *Fisher house, ca. 1855*

5

5. *Methodist Church, 1842*

6. *Back of the Methodist Church*

One door farther down Main Street, and one door farther down even than that, are two public buildings which are, again, simple rectangular boxes, but detailed and ornamented in special ways that signal their importance in the town. The Methodist Church, built in 1842 and paid for mostly by whaling captains, is organized like a very large barn. (5) Inside on the ground floor is a series of small meeting rooms. The main meeting room, the church, is in, as it were, the loft. But the effect from the front is of only one story, not two. With its high portico and triangular pediment supported by six gigantic wood columns, the building is made to seem less like a barn and more like a classical temple reborn on Main Street. There is a commonsense economy here, too, for on the back of the church where the message seems less urgent, all pretensions have been abandoned. There is no cornice, no pediment, and no decorations—only four windows to let in the light, and two utilitarian brick chimneys. (6)

The form of the church, a box, provides a place for people to sit and listen and talk as part of a deliberately simple ceremony. But the care and energy its builders spent on embellishing the form—in the portico and, separately, in the tower which finally was graced with little Gothic spires—serves an equally important function. These embellishments proclaim, with a set of symbols recognizable to all, the place of the church in the life of the community.

The symbols of the courthouse next door on Main Street are more subdued. The size of the whole building and its scale—that is, the relative size of its windows, doors, and portico—are both smaller than those of the church. Perhaps to seem more enduring the courthouse is built of brick, but strangely its effect is not much less domestic than that of any house in Edgartown. (7)

7. Dukes County Courthouse, ca. 1840

8. The length of Main Street

9. Lower Main Street

All four of these buildings—the two houses, the church, and the courthouse—are essentially similar. Each is a set of greater or lesser rooms put together to make a box with a roof on top. When it was deemed appropriate, various decorations were put on the outside surfaces. Because these buildings were made in similar ways by people with similar attitudes, they are all good neighbors. But because each was made for a different reason, each has its special meaning. The two houses reflect two families' very different senses of themselves (Captain Snow is said to have paid for his house with profits from selling his wife's homemade candy). The church and the courthouse, one very grand and the other surprisingly modest, tell something not just about churches and courthouses, but about their relationship to the town.

Main Street runs from the flagpole downhill to the harbor. It thus has a well-defined beginning and end. (8) This is the principal commercial street in Edgartown, though there are houses and institutional buildings all along it. At the lower end of the street the commercial buildings are woven together into a dense fabric. Each of them encloses something of its own, an office or a shop or a bank. Together they all help enclose the street itself by making walls on either side of it. The buildings here seem almost to have been eroded by the continuous stream of pedestrian traffic along their fronts. The shops, which people enter most, have glassy display windows and deep-set doors which invite entrance. The offices, resisting erosion more, have smaller windows and doors which simply open onto the street and look as though they allow access only when necessary. (9)

One block above the harbor, Main Street intersects Water Street at a ninety-degree angle. This is Four Corners, the crossroads of Edgartown. Its special importance is acknowledged by two of the stores on it, which have their entrances not on either street, but opening to the corner itself. (10) Water Street runs roughly parallel to the harbor to the northern and southern outskirts of Edgartown. Near Four Corners it is the second most important commercial street in the town and, particularly on the north side, the most prominent residential street as well.

North Water Street is where some of Edgartown's earliest houses were built, and one of the finest collections of eighteenth- and early nineteenth-century houses in New England can be found on it a few blocks away from Four Corners. At first there were no houses on the harbor side of the street, and so the lots on the opposite side, where the most impressive houses are, had a commanding view of the harbor. Between Simpson's Lane and Morse Street are four elegantly simple houses of big and dominant shapes, jumbled close together to stake a strong claim on their spare pieces of ground and, together, to front the street.

The houses are skewed with respect to one another, since two of them are built parallel to the street and two parallel to their skewed lot lines—in order, according to local tradition, to allow their original owners to observe incoming ships. (11) Though they are considerably bigger and have very carefully made doorways or porches, these houses were put together in the same manner as the Joshua Snow house at the top of Main Street. Each is a wooden box sheathed in white clapboards or shingles, with windows that can be shuttered off; each is separated from the street and sidewalk by a white picket fence, which breaks at the front door to allow entrance. The modest differences between these houses are signaled by the merest variations in detail—here a

10. Four Corners

11. North Water Street

9

12. Houses on North Water and Morse streets

13. Site plan of three houses on North Water Street

14. Houses on North Water Street

hip rather than a gable roof, here double sash windows with twelve panes of glass over twelve rather than six over six, and here an especially elaborate front door.

A little farther out North Water Street there are two houses, one on either side of the intersection with Morse Street, which are much grander in execution and indicate a more extensive awareness of the site and its view of the harbor. Each is pushed close to the street, each is entered from the side street, and each has a porch of considerable grandeur on the Water Street side. These houses with their imposing porches do more than face the harbor. They have been built consciously to give particular importance and animation to Water Street. We use a special word to describe their relation to it. The houses *enfront* Water Street, formally and respectfully. (12) The actual entrances on Morse Street, in contrast, look downright modest.

One of these two houses forms a trio with its immediate neighbors to the north. The house immediately next door is set far back on its deep lot, with a front lawn on Water Street and a fenced-in path across the back of the corner lot to a gate on Morse Street. In this way this house and the one on the corner both have access to both streets and, more importantly, each gains light and outlook across the other's yard. (13) The house which is now set far back was originally close to Water Street. Half a century ago it was moved, so that it and the house on the corner (as well as the third house to the north) share an uncommon reciprocity.

Third in the trio is perhaps the grandest and most powerful house on the street. The open space it shares with the other two allows its power to be more fully appreciated, as well as giving its owners the chance to survey the activities of the street from a position secured by carefully trimmed hedges and to enjoy the open air and surrounding green. (14)

Farther out, North Water Street jogs abruptly and becomes Starbuck Neck Road. This turn and the change of name correspond to a complete transformation in the nature of the street. The extension of the road was made in the nineteenth century, and most of the houses along it date from the period around the turn of the twentieth.

To the landward side of the road an overtly modern house of the 1950s retreats into a clump of pine trees and merges with them. Its stained wood siding and large areas of glass are barely discernible through the tree branches, mostly because, like the branches, they establish a pattern that is textural rather than volumetric. Thus, the house stands in strong contrast to the intensely communal interactions of the earlier, denser town, and, like most of the other houses farther down the road, it offers little to the street on which it is placed.

Also on the landward side of the road is a house which does many things at once. As a softly contoured and weathered shape it merges with its land. Yet on its corner is a high tower, which strongly marks the place of the house in its surroundings. And the tower, with its evocations of dominance and display, is complemented by the deep-set porch along the front of the house, with its ancient suggestion of caves. All these things have more to do with an extension into a private psychic realm than with the agreed-upon patterns of public and private interaction developed on Main and North Water streets. (15)

The houses on the ocean side are set far back from the road and attend not to it but to the open meadows of beach grass, to the sand, and to the sea beyond. (16) Their big volumetric shapes take hold of more land

15. *House on Starbuck Neck Road, ca. 1885*

16. *Houses on Starbuck Neck Road from the water*

than the tightly spaced houses on North Water Street. Their gray shingled sides are punctured by bays and porches which both extend shelter to the out-of-doors and breathe the sea air into the balloonlike forms of the buildings.

Water Street and Main Street cut cross axes through the fabric of Edgartown and provide a psychically comforting structure; you always know where you are, or at least what you are near. The town is thus mapped out quite simply: you are either on one of the principal streets or in a quadrant of the town defined by them.

The two main streets also are the settings for a large number of man-made things— churches, stores, banks, hotels, and houses. Few of these are very big, and none dwarfs any of the others. No matter what their size they were all built in a traditionally accepted way, sufficiently clear to have been understood by everyone and sufficiently flexible to have allowed for variations in need and desire.

Edgartown is not just a collection of separate things, but something memorable in itself. It seems that in doing what he needed to do for himself, each builder also managed to do something for the whole town; the result is at once unified and energetically various. Many of the striking variations in any part of the town seem to have been appreciated by the neighbors and echoed in a burst of friendly assent. There is on North Water Street not just one cater-cornered house but several, and on Starbuck Neck Road not just one house set back but five.

On Davis Lane there is another special collection of houses which express another sort of common consent. These houses are small, but they stake powerful claims on their sites by using every inch of them. One of these is a model of the way even a tiny house can make the land around it thor-

oughly its own. The lot is scarcely half again as big as the house, and every part of it has been intensely developed—as intensely, one imagines, as the inside of the house itself. The other houses next door on Davis Lane occupy their sites with a similar energy. (17)

North of Main Street, near the corner of Cottage and Fuller Streets, are several houses created in a different way. These houses are alike only in their eccentricity. Here most of them are set back from the street on fairly generous lots, and nearly all of them seem to have responded in some spirited way to one or another of the stylistic revivals which were fashionable in the nineteenth century.

The house on the corner of the two streets, for example, seems to have first been built like any other house in Edgartown. In its original form it was probably not unlike the Joshua Snow house, but at a later date, probably around 1870, it was Gothicized by the addition of a new façade and a dormer in the middle of the roof and details, like the elegant barge boards which curve along the roof line. (18) Thus what was originally one kind of house for one kind of family became, by a transmutation of images, another kind of house for another family— one with different dreams about what their house should be. The owners of the house across the street followed the lead and applied Gothic details to their house as well, but unfortunately they lacked some of the panache of their more adventurous neighbors.

Not too far away, on Winter Street, is a house which owes something to the Greek Revival style, which advocated the scholarly application of details from classical architecture to public and private buildings. (19) This house, again, is a simple story-and-a-half box, to which Doric columns and heavy cornices and pediments have been applied,

17. Houses on Davis Lane, nineteenth century

18. Gothic cottage, nineteenth century

19. House on Winter Street, ca. 1835

20. *House on Durham Road, nineteenth century*

21. *Twin houses on Durham road, mid-twentieth century*

here with more enthusiasm than scholarship, for the columns are irregularly spaced across the front, influenced more by the off-center front door than by the principles of symmetry. The columns themselves, as well as the other details, are wrought surprisingly large for a building so small, and are awkward and strange, like full-grown toes on a half-grown puppy. The sheer energy of the effort, though, however haphazardly it manifests itself, produced a good-natured success.

Down South Water Street, at the edge of the harbor along Durham Road, there is an instructive juxtaposition of the old and the new. The old house at the end of Durham Road seems to have begun life, like so many other houses in Edgartown, as a box with a simple gable roof. Later, a series of additions were made, probably by a different family, which changed its character. On the front were added another dormer window, placed eccentrically to the right, a two-story octagonal bay on the left corner, and a deep porch all across the front. The new part of the house is shingled, whereas the old part still shows its clapboards. (20) In a casual and homely way, the house tells of a family's active effort to lay their own special claim on an older house of which they found themselves the owners.

Two modern houses up the street are built on the same lot, one forward of the other in a way reminiscent of the trio on North Water Street. (21) With their shingles and white trim they rather self-consciously recall earlier ways of building on the Vineyard. But their import seems embarrassingly limited, perhaps because the once wide area of agreement about how to build a house has shrunk considerably in the twentieth century, or perhaps because architects' methods of communicating their clients' desires through draftsmen to builders leaves many relationships unnoticed and many problems unsolved.

These houses, too, obviously have exactly the same floor plan, flipped without change, even though their relationships to the street are altogether different. The automatic repetition leaves room for such anomalies as the spaces under the upper front decks—not garages, apparently, since the pavement bypasses them; not terraces either, for there is no opening to the room inside. It doesn't seem unrealistic to suppose that these spaces simply appeared when the houses were built, without anyone having realized that they would be there.

If the conscious attempts of these houses to "fit" into their surroundings make us uneasy by their lack of success, then another twentieth-century house on the other side of the town might drive us to despair. (22) It is every inch "Colonial," meant to look just like the other houses in Edgartown. But it bears about as much resemblance to them as Little Orphan Annie, with her round and empty eyes, does to real people. The front door looks as if it were always meant to be closed. Could any life ever shine through those undersized, blanked-out windows? Everything here is perfunctory, stereotypical. The details, windows, and doors all seem to have been ordered over the telephone. Each piece of the house feels a little too small. No detail reflects any particular concern; it all looks like a general solution, something an early computer might have come up with if it had been assigned a "Colonial" to do in an aggressively post-Colonial epoch. This house has received little, and is giving little in return. A good house needs active support, prideful originality, or at least prideful concern.

In three hundred years, Edgartown has spawned a succession of houses in very close agreement to one another without any two

22. *A mid-twentieth-century house*

17

23. Houses in Oak Bluffs, ca. 1875

houses being exactly alike. Perfunctory attempts to "fit" tastefully risk being lifeless, since care, like love, has to be felt personally and delivered personally and cannot yet be simulated in the catalogue or in the lumber yard.

It is worth noting, though, and it is dramatically revealed a few miles up the road from Edgartown, in Oak Bluffs, that there are many kinds of caring, including the romantic, wistful, maybe even silly attempt to give body to a dream of another place and time. (23)

Oak Bluffs was built all at once in the 1870s as a place for families to spend the summer by the sea in Methodist transport. Tiny Gothic houses scaled well below life size, a paleo-Disneyland, are arranged in a grand plan around greenswards on which giant tabernacles stood and still stand. The houses, so good-natured and so winsomely funny, appear to be exploring the structural limits of gingerbread, but their Hänsel-and-Gretel connotation is only surface; they have a multilayered richness that is generic to fairy tales from the northern forests.

Miraculously, the little romantic houses are not silly. They are graced by the special attention which went into their meticulous details, and by a common spirit which informs each individual house.

Generations of community assent have built Edgartown; Oak Bluffs came into being all at once, and outside the agreements of nineteenth-century society. Yet it is as much a *place*, as memorable and special, as the one built over the centuries.

Santa Barbara

Overhead, above the flickering light of a movie, incandescent stars glow brighter than smog would ever allow. On either side of the cinema screen is the façade of an Andalusian village. Its windows, doors, and balconies, its stairs and loggias seem as though they were about to be peopled by bright throngs dancing to the festive rhythms of old Spain.

The matinee ends, the stars are flicked off, and we walk outside into the arcades of the Fox Arlington Theatre and the benign breezes of Southern California. Straight ahead a broad, timbered roof shades the center of the passage. Under it a tiled fountain splashes, and to each side are gardens open to the sky. They are bounded, like much of Santa Barbara, by blank white walls, with sun and shadow dappling their surfaces. (1) The whole scene has the relaxed air of a Mediterranean dream. At the front of the theater a delicate wrought-iron box office and the tranquil arcades that open to the street contrast sharply with contemporary clamor across the way. There the heraldic red, white, and blue of a Standard Oil gas station jousts in commercial battle with the orange and black of a neighboring Union 76.

Santa Barbara's most characteristic buildings, like the Fox, were built shortly after the devastating earthquake of 1925. And although life has changed since then, the town still has an apparent coherence that owes nearly everything to the deliberate imposition of a Mediterranean style on its main streets and public buildings when they were rebuilt. (2) The Mediterranean dream so engaged the imagination of Santa Barbara's citizens that forty years later the refurbishing of State Street, the main shopping artery, was executed fully within the spirit of the original intentions.

Buildings in the Spanish tradition are by no means to be found everywhere in Santa Barbara, though they do make up most of State Street and segments of the suburbs. Major public buildings give impetus to the style and confirm its dominance.

In Santa Barbara, houses, shops, and even movie theaters and the courthouses sustain a common imagery—they seem convincingly of one place even though they are separated in location. This coherence is not maintained

1. *Arcade of the Fox Arlington Theatre, ca. 1930*

2. *State Street*

just by "style," by white walls, tile roofs, and black wrought-iron grilles. It is fundamentally created by a characteristic relationship between people and enclosure.

At almost every point in the town one is conscious of being enclosed—of being next to walls or within spaces with touchable limits. (3) In the splendid climate these walls don't need to be roofed. Often they form outdoor rooms as clearly defined as any inside. The walls of Santa Barbara are an accompaniment to one's movement, a recurring beat that measures passage from place to place. The spaces between are given life by sunlight and darkness, bright windows, shaded arcades, shimmering tiles, the shadows of iron grilles, and exuberant leaves. These walls, open stairways, balconies, and arcades throughout the town serve to symbolize, as much as actually to invite the movement of people between indoors and out. (4) They are an affirmation that the public realm is as much to be lived in as the private. By encouraging and dramatizing the act of public habitation, the builders of Santa Barbara have made a stage for daily action and encounter as rich as any devised by Hollywood.

These riches have been embodied most vividly in places like El Paseo, a labyrinth of courtyards, passages, and open rooms that house many small shops, a few second-level offices, and a splendid balconied restaurant open to the sky. The complex (5), built just before the earthquake of 1925, is a dramatic example of the *assumption* of style. The "Street in Spain," bounded by glowing white walls and colorful awnings, slips between two historic adobes built in the early nineteenth century. (6) These have been incorporated into the shopping compound and set the tone for its fundamental domesticity.

Several other shopping passages also run

3. Wall on Mission Street

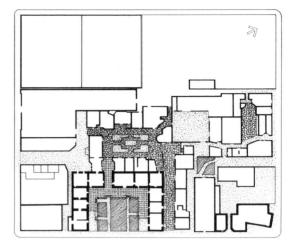

5. Plan of El Paseo, by James Osborne Craig, 1925

4. Copper Coffee Pot, by Edwards, Plunkett, and Howells, ca. 1930

6. "Street in Spain," El Paseo

from State Street through buildings into
enclosed courtyards surrounded by loggias
and greenery. Together these make a network of pedestrian passages through the
town. Along them, as along the streets,
many buildings wear the familiar emblems
of domesticity—awnings, balconies, and
doors and windows scaled to human size.
(7) These elements are basic to Santa Barbara's architecture. In many recent buildings
they have been almost completely lost, and a
bogus tile-roofed style has developed—an
emasculated institutional classicism which is
a good deal less humane than the earlier
tradition. (8)

The most dramatically rich examples from
the twenties are the Fox Arlington Theatre
and the Santa Barbara County Court House.
(9) The latter is an extraordinary interweaving of accessibility and grandeur—a
palace that is open to the people and re-
splendent with tiles, woodcarving, and wall
painting in long open-air passages that
adjoin a very large courtyard. This yard
is open on one and a half sides to the town,
but has a ceremonial entrance through an
arch that seems scaled to the mountains
behind it. (10) The court is focused on a
dramatic set of terraces with a heroic stair-
landing at stage-center. (11) This is a cul-
mination, in magnificent civic scale, of the
dream that created this part of Santa Barbara, an Anglo-Californian vision of Spanish
romance traced against the ever-present
whitewashed walls.

The houses most clearly a part of the
Santa Barbara dream are concentrated in
outlying sections of town. The houses on
Mesa and Middle roads in Montecito reveal
both the power of this vernacular and the
variety that can be achieved within it. (12)
The general environs are richly tropical,
with eucalyptus, oak, and pepper trees,
thick ground cover, and particularly tall

7. *State Street*

8. *State Street*

9. Santa Barbara County Court House, by William Mooser, 1929

11. Courtyard, Santa Barbara County Court House

10. Entrance, Santa Barbara County Court House

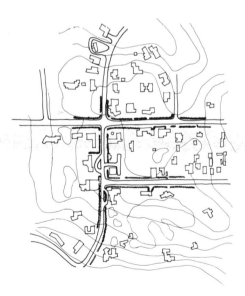

12. Plan of Mesa Road (vertical) and Middle Road (top horizontal), Montecito

13. Mesa Road

14. Gateway on Mesa Road

flowering plants. (13) Along Mesa Road dense hedges and white walls enclose the street and establish protected courtyards between each house and the road. (14)

The continuous accompaniment provided by walls downtown has here a softer, but still recognizable rhythm. The interspersed hedges and walls enclose all space, sheltering the private realms and giving habitable shape to the public space of the road. Sometimes the space between house and road is formed by a hedge and occupied by various species of grandiloquent plants. (15) In other cases the style is not the same, but the format is constant, as in the example of an earlier Mission-style house. (16) The fundamental staging is the same: road, forecourt, and then house, with the entire property surrounded and screened from the street.

The characteristics of this Mission-style house stand in marked contrast to the next house along the street. It is entirely alien to its surroundings. (17) It has neither the fundamental relationship of indoors to out, nor even the superficial stylistic trappings of architecture in Santa Barbara. It is rude to its neighbors. It is set back and removed from the road to which it offers nothing but a driveway loop, clipped ivy, and the tail-ends of fat cars. It neither enfronts the street nor surrounds the site. It is pallid and indeterminate. Its long, extended eaves and the gentle slope of its roof seem clearly intended to merge with a site made up of highways and prairies. It should have been in Illinois; here in Santa Barbara it cuts into and partially destroys the special characteristics of the street.

The hospitable sheltering afforded by the street is restored, however, around the corner on Middle Road, where white walls, hedges, trees, and gate posts mark out a public thoroughfare in a residential setting. (18) It is the allegiance of all the houses on

15. *House on Mesa Road*

17. *House on Mesa Road*

16. *House on Mesa Road*

18. *Middle Road*

19. House on Middle Road

20. Heberton house, Middle Road, by George Washington Smith, 1916

the street to a common format that creates this neighborly success.

The strength of the format is undiminished by some of the eccentricities which occur beyond the edge of the street. The courtyard of one house in particular (19) is aloof from human action, like the set for a science-fiction movie. Sleek autos slide behind white seamless doors (automated, no doubt) and leave the blacktopped courtyard in the care of two concrete squirrels. These childish white figures serve, perhaps, as symbols outside of an atrophied dream life within— condemned to the air-conditioned splendor of Saturday morning cartoons on the tube.

Directly across the street is a house which is a more notable success. (20) Though it is quite different from the other houses on Middle Road, it still adheres in its own way to the common format. This house was at one time the home of George Washington Smith, the architect who designed much of what we now admire in Santa Barbara. It enfronts the street directly. The wall that in other instances would be the courtyard is here the wall of the house itself. There is no intermediate space whatsoever, yet the whole house becomes a boundary to the street and the entry to the site beyond. On the inside is a row of rooms that open through glass doors and large windows onto a deep garden behind the house. On the street front the white stucco façade serves as an edge for the street as definitively as do the hedges and trees along the rest of the road. Above the front door, on the second floor, a pair of glass doors lead onto a shallow balcony with elaborate wrought-iron railings decorated with geraniums. This little symbol, like the awnings and balconies of the commercial buildings on State Street, and unlike the anonymous, automated house across the street, signals the presence of people. Have those doors ever been opened?

Has anyone ever appeared on the balcony except to water the plants? The answers are probably not very important; symbols of habitation can be almost as effective as human presence itself in giving empty stages an air of life.

Just at the corner of Mesa and Middle roads another house by George Washington Smith is perhaps the most graceful of the group. (21) Its entrance courtyard is formed on two sides by the house and on the others by thick, artfully trimmed hedges, which separate the house from the two streets. The surface of the court is gravel, used for the most part as a driveway. In the center a stone-paved circle with a statue and potted plants marks a path for cars and focuses attention. The rest of the courtyard, with a richly carved entrance door, carefully trimmed vines and an array of luxuriant plants, serves as further evidence of the individual attention and care that can flourish within the accepted format of this place.

The estate began life by adopting an old tradition and continues life by accommodating changing conditions. The building behind the house—between it and the first George Washington Smith house—has been converted into a separate dwelling, and a wing of the house opening directly onto Mesa Road has been converted into an apartment. The side garden, moreover, which originally extended all the way to Oak Road, has been broken up to provide a site for a newer house on the corner of Oak Road and Mesa Road. But the tremendous resource that the garden represented has been respected and used. A long allée of trees, for instance, and the original side gate have been transformed into the entry court for the modest new house. (22) It stands as an indeterminate white block almost invisible—still according to the format—behind the existing hedges. There could hardly be a more eloquent

21. *Smith house, Mesa and Middle Roads, by George Washington Smith, 1920*

22. *Gateway, Smith house, Oak Road*

27

23. Entrance, Faculty Club, University of California at Santa Barbara, by Moore, Lyndon, Turnbull, Whitaker (MLTW)/ Moore—Turnbull, 1961

25. Courtyard, Faculty Club

24. Rotunda, Faculty Club

26. Dining Room, Faculty Club

example of adaptation by simple means, inspired by a sensitivity to the immediate surroundings and to the characteristic spirit of the place.

Our own encounter with the traditions of Santa Barbara came when we were asked to design a Faculty Club—half-house, half-public building—for the University of California there. The development of the campus had been subject to a restrictive set of architectural controls that were meant to bring the institutional style of the existing campus, built in the fifties, into some harmony with the imagery of Santa Barbara. We thought the polite repertoire of red tile roofs, muted colors, and decorative concrete blocks lacked the theatrical spirit of Santa Barbara's exuberant civic recreation of a past that had really never existed.

To make this place a part of the Santa Barbara fantasy we thought it necessary to build within the accepted format, but with some latter-day spirit. The building became a set of walled enclosures, indoors and out. The walls are white, shadowed by one another and interwoven with heavy wood timbers. There are stairs and measured openings to dramatize the public actions of its inhabitants.

The blank entrance wall of the club is pushed close against the abutting service road. The entrance itself ramps up through a simple planted forecourt to an opening between the walls. (23) Passing through a covered, but unenclosed segment of the building one comes upon a dizzily inverted set of curving walls that serve as vestibule to the open courts within. (24) On three sides these courts are bounded by high white walls with openings cut into them to form loggias. (25) Passing along the upper court one enters another vestibule, this one enclosed.

Inside, from the midlevel entry, is a view down onto the chairs and tables of the main dining room and up to the peak of the great room. (26) The room is spanned by walled trusses that fan up from the far corner of the low wall to a high point forty-two feet above the floor on the opposite wall. A broad, simple stair descends into the main space, and a bridge crosses to lounges on the other side. There additional stairs twist erratically up into the private attic bar at the top. These stairs and bridges, like the exterior stairs and balconies in the buildings of the town, add life to this public room by putting stage-center the comings and goings of club members.

The backgrounds for all this are the stucco walls—in this case two layers. The inner wall serves, usually, to hold windows and doors. The outer wall, with large, syncopated openings is meant as a buffer for the sun, protecting the interior from intrusion by subtropical rays, though letting occasional beams of light animate the space by sliding across upper walls far above human reach. (27)

All this was built two generations after the heyday of agreement about the Santa Barbara style, so its qualities are a little less "Spanish" and a little thinner and stagier than those of the courthouse. But we hope that it shares some of its *brio* and gains strength from participating in the agreement.

Santa Barbara is less than a hundred miles from Los Angeles, one of the world's largest and most expansive floating environmental crap games, a place characterized by minimum agreement about anything. Los Angeles's millions and its murk are approaching along the freeways. So far, the special magic of Santa Barbara remains virtually undiminished, partly because so much care and agreement have been expended on it, and partly because the physical embodiment of the shared dream is so

29

27. Exterior, Faculty Club

splendidly protective of itself. A city of walls, hedges, and trees, with mountains for a distant view, where buildings generally merge into their sites, can withstand violations.

Even with such armaments it is probably only a question of time before Santa Barbara's quiet splendors are submerged. But while they last, they are eloquent testimony to the power of human imagination, even when it is imagining a history that never was. Robert Frost talked of fences; the Japanese seek order and beauty in the shadows. In Santa Barbara, a dream is sheltered by hedges and walls, and expanded by continuous images of human habitation.

The Sea Ranch

In 1965, a new second-home community called the Sea Ranch was begun along the California coast a hundred miles north of San Francisco. It was widely acclaimed for its ecologically sound architecture and for its concern for planning the organic environment. Because the Sea Ranch is so impressively full of good intentions, because it has had a great deal of influence, because the influence it has had is so roundly abominated for a number of valid reasons, and because we designed part of it, we add its case to those of Edgartown and Santa Barbara, to develop further our notion of a livable community and the place of houses in it. Unlike the first two towns, the Sea Ranch presents a particularly modern set of problems, and unrequited hopes, and failures.

The intentions were splendid: Oceanic Properties, the real estate subsidiary of one of the Hawaiian "Big Five" companies, Castle & Cooke, bought 5,000 acres along ten spectacular miles of coast well past the San Francisco metropolitan and vacation areas. Oceanic was financially able to plan a community which might be developed slowly and "properly" without the usually frantic developers' concern for instant profits.

The Oceanic Properties vice president in charge of the project, Alfred Boeke, hired as landscape architects the firm of Lawrence Halprin and Associates, whose geographer made exhaustive and very helpful studies of the local ecology and problems of wind, weather, and site. To make architectural prototypes for development based on these studies, Joseph Esherick was retained to design clustered houses and a store. We, then the firm of Moore, Lyndon, Turnbull, Whitaker, were asked to plan for even tighter clustering of houses in condominiums along the shore. Because our work as architects had been primarily residential, the Sea Ranch was a welcome chance for us to develop ideas we had been putting to use in individual houses.

These ideas began with the premise that the architect *particularizes*. He discerns special patterns of human activity, and organizes movement. He develops a clarifying pattern, a design to which the whole process of building is subjected. Within this pattern there must be a controlling image that gives people the chance to know where they are—in space, in time, and in the order of things. People must have something to be in.

Thus the fundamental principle of architecture is territorial. The architect assembles physical materials from which the observer creates not just an image of a building but of "place."

All this implies that there be distinctions between "inside" and "outside." The modulation from one to the other is, and always has been, one of the primary elements of the architect's art.

For some time we had been especially concerned with making several *degrees* of "inside," marking first a place in the landscape, then progressively segregating places outdoors and in, so that the user could be continually aware of his location, from the altogether natural and unprotected outside to the sheltered, secluded, and protected inside.

The Sea Ranch was built on a wild exposed coast. Before Oceanic's arrival, the landscape was grand and very simple. The top of bluffs along the shore form a coastal plain only a few hundred yards wide. (1) Beyond that there is a ridge of low hills. The entire site was originally covered with redwood and bishop pine, but had been logged in the 1890s on the seaward slope. When we began work, the upper areas were covered with seventy-year-old second growth, but the treeless land from below the crest to the edge of the bluff had been extensively grazed by sheep.

The most arresting features of the landscape were the fifty-year-old belts of Monterey cypress introduced perpendicular to the coast at irregular intervals for wind protection. The cool wind from the northeast is an almost constant factor here, though the place is relatively free from the fog in which most of California's north coast is often shrouded.

The major problem for human habitation was to get out of the wind and into sunlight. The absence of places to do this (except for the cypress hedgerows) lent an air of splendid desolation to the site, as it does indeed to the whole north coast.

The isolation and the haunting beauty of the land made development an awesome proposition. Houses which merged politely into the land would seem to provide little sense of security on this wild coast. Houses which stood out too strongly would emasculate those very astringencies which made the land special. What we and Esherick thought was needed was a limited partnership—not a marriage—between the buildings and the land. Then we developed ways of building that we thought would be responsive to the particulars of the site and climate.

Our own structure was made of heavy wood frames with windows big enough to let in the sunshine (but never so high that the salt spray couldn't be washed off) and skylights overhead, with rough wood enclosures surrounding smooth ones to multiply the implications of "inside." Any landscaped outdoors was walled into inclusion as a part of the "inside," so as not to impinge on the wild landscape (in a partnership one must be very careful of what is whose). It leaves the wild landscape, right up to the walls of the houses, unspoiled, and uncluttered with lawn chairs or flower beds.

The site chosen for the condominium was a grassy, windswept field bordering a rocky shore where the waves break high against the cliffs. (2) It is a place at once barren, rugged, and grand. Because the condominium was big (ten times the size of a house), we were able to match the building to the

1. The Pacific coast at the Sea Ranch

2. Condominium, by MLTW, 1966

3. Cluster houses (in background), by Joseph Esherick, 1966

4. Condominium

large scale of the site. Limited to the design of small individual houses, Esherick made his buildings recede into the landscape. (3)

Our designs and Esherick's were not at all coordinated. We were eager, in fact, to keep our responses to the accumulating environmental data as independent as we could, so as to avoid a contrived "style." But as it turned out, the conditions were so stringent that Esherick's houses and our original condominium developed an idiom surprisingly similar, of shed roofs to deflect the wind with no overhangs for the wind to flutter—and with generous windows punched low in walls of vertical redwood boards. (4)

All this was in the narrow sense functional. The Sea Ranch condominium, unlike the buildings in Santa Barbara, was not meant to look "like" anything in particular, though of course it did look like all sorts of things. People recognized similarities between the condominium and old buildings on mining and timbering sites. Since we have been enthusiasts for barns and country industrial structures, we were pleased, though the resemblance was not intentional. But we were at odds with critics who, for some reason, considered such resemblance unwarranted.

The condominium building was the initial attempt to make a community. It consists of ten great rooms with tower, courts, bays, and solaria (5), ranged around two common courtyards—a first layer of "inside." (6) Like the coves it overlooks on either side, its inner courtyard is surrounded by forms which slope to the sea, countered by an occasional projection. (7) At once castle, compound, and promontory, it is a concentration of dwellings bunched together in the teeth of the wind.

Inside each dwelling there is a powerful need for further domestication, for another

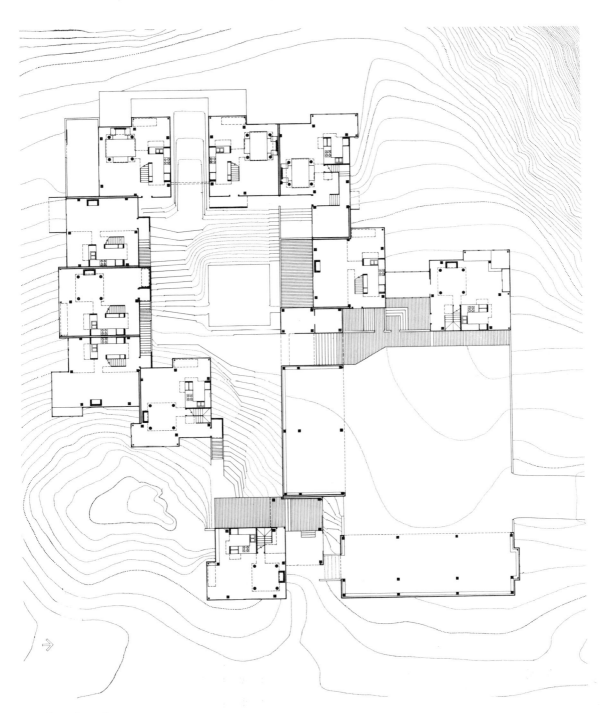

5. Plan of condominium

6. *Courtyard, condominium*

7. *Exterior, condominium*

layer of shelter and a sense of being yet farther "inside," though not out of sight of the crashing surf. Every dwelling is composed of a single great room (8), and almost every one of these contains two little houses, one of them a simple four-posted shelter covering a hearth and supporting a bed-chamber on top. (9) The other is almost a miniature house which contains a kitchen below, a bath and dressing room above, and sometimes a sleeping loft above that. (10) The outer structure of the encompassing room is built of large rough pieces of wood visibly deployed as in a barn to stiffen the structure against the elements. (11) The little houses inside are made of smooth wood, and generally painted, so that they seem miniature, something between toy houses and giant cabinets. Around the periphery, bays reach out to special views or to provide extra places for sitting or sleeping, conceptually "outside" the envelope of the house, bracingly close to the windy outdoors. (12)

Each of the dwellings is different, to suit its particular position on the site or to provide auxiliary sleeping rooms or galleries or solaria. (13) Unit 9, for instance, has a small wooden entry and eating court and a glass-walled porch (14) outside the great room on the south and a long bay that hangs out over the cliff on the west and north. The kitchen/bath house cabinet has been painted in five shades of blue to distinguish it from the rough exposed wood framing and wall surfaces around. A ladder up its side from the second floor leads to a loft above the bathroom, from which the agile can supervise the scene below. (15)

The entire place becomes a large, but still measurable foil to the limitless Pacific horizon outside. At floor level you can examine both: you can move about within the room which is peopled with columns

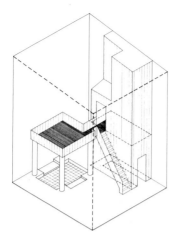

8. *Typical condominium unit*

9. *Typical condominium four-poster*

10. *Typical condominium kitchen and bath*

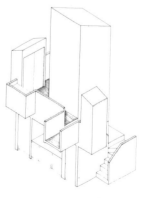

11. *Condominium structural detail*

13. *Solarium, condominium unit 1*

12. *Bay window and living room, condominium
unit 9*

14. *Glass porch, condominium unit 9*

15. *Kitchen and bath block, condominium unit 9*

and posts, then stretch out in bays with views of the outdoors or the inside. You will always be next to tactile elements of the room's structure, or protected just beyond its boundaries, conscious at once of the overwhelming outdoors and the sheltered room within. (16)

The land planning for the Sea Ranch was carried on by Halprin's landscape designers, who wanted to maintain the brooding qualities of the site even though they knew that the lonely sweep of coast must eventually be carved into parcels which could be bought and sold.

In the forest, the problems were readily surmountable; handsome roads were slipped in among the trees, sites with some forest amenity or a view were selected, lot lines were drawn around them, and houses built. Almost automatically these houses have merged into their sites with the forest close around them. (17)

In the meadows, on the other hand, the problems were far more difficult. Land close to the water was so valuable it had to be sold, though it was clear to everyone that the *sense* of openness of the meadows between the hedgerows had to be preserved. The management did not think it would be possible to build more houses in the right places near the hedgerows with the kind of care that had been lavished on the Esherick clusters. But in order to exercise some control, the developer saw to it that more than half the meadowland remained in common ownership. Much of the other half marked for sale was placed in a "private restricted zone" which cannot be built upon. This left only about one-fourth of the meadowland available for building and, in the first meadows, the attempt was made to have those building sites relate to the hedgerows.

Another aspect of the land planning which

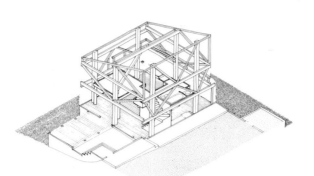

16. Condominium unit 9

18. Fort Ross, Sonoma County, California, ca. 1812

17. Hines house, by MLTW/Moore–Turnbull, 1966

received careful initial attention from the consultants was a set of design restrictions. The phrase rankled, but there seemed to be some point in making a booklet full of the information about the site which we had found useful. The only rigid proscription was against reflective surfaces and bright colors (and we were later sorry even for those). We did not want restrictions that would back the designer into a set scheme; what we wanted was something that would encourage a rich multiplicity of images, each of them closely dependent on the land. We did not get it.

A look at the place seven years later is instructive: the care lavished on it by so many people makes it worth our attention, and its successes and failures should give some clear clues to the present-day place of houses.

The land is still beautiful as one drives up the coast from San Francisco. The chapel of the Russian settlement at Fort Ross (18), which had been skillfully restored in the 1950s, had spoken eloquently of the power over the mind exercised by a small outpost at the lonely edge of the world; it had had a strong hold on us, when the Sea Ranch was starting. Now it has been burned to the ground by vandals, and in the wholesale manner of the seventies the state is talking of restoring an entire Russian village.

After Fort Ross the coast is wooded and the road winding, and it is some time before we spot (because we know where to look) the silhouette of our condominium, "like a large wooden rock," as one of our friends had put it. (19) When we get closer, though, we note that another condominium is under way hard behind it. (20) Its architect appears to be unfriendly, at least, to the scale of the "wooden rock" on the land, since he has suppressed the hillock with a building all

19. Coastline with condominium

20. New condominium

41

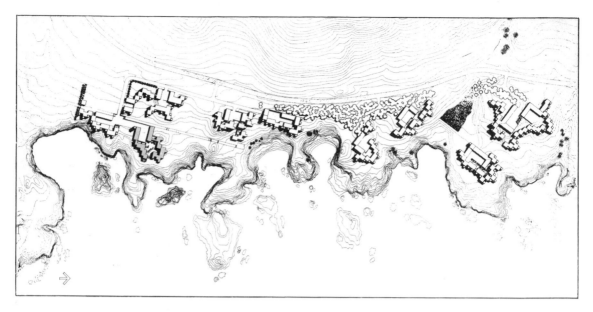

21. Original site plans for condominiums

22. Entrance to lodge and condominiums; lodge right,
old condominium left, new condominium adjacent.

jagged and frilly, and it looms large for so
petulant a structure.

The original site plan (21) had arranged
condominiums like the first down the whole
narrow stretch of coast in careful relation
to one another and to the land. This building seems to be ignoring the plan and the
intentions behind it (as well as the view
itself). It turns out that the condominium
program was delayed and did not continue
past the first building because the salesmen
on the site could make their 6 percent fees
much more quickly on vacant land, without
more investment by Oceanic Properties and
without the trouble and complexity of showing dwellings already built. They pressed
for five years to delay condominium construction, and the present work is going on
only because a contractor bought some land
and brought his architect from the ski
country to fashion this chalet. The residents
are angry. They are also powerless.

Adjoining the condominiums, just past
the gate (22), is a lodge which has swallowed
up the original 1965 Esherick store. It is
handsomely built in what is by now the Sea
Ranch vernacular. But it doesn't seem quite
right, probably because it is not observing
that meticulous *quid pro quo* with the wild
environment that the first building had;
its parking lot sprawls, and it even has little
lawns making inroads into the flammable
high grass. The trouble, probably, is that
it is too much in the Sea Ranch image, a
vernacular based on loneliness. Even on the
parking lot side, where many people move,
it is still mute, as if it faced the empty
fields. From a distance, nevertheless, its
sizeable bulk sits easily on the ground.

Look, however, at that excrescence on the
grassy slopes above the meadow. (23) It had
long been evident that buildings there would
destroy the shape of the land, but new in-
house land planning, pressed harder and

23. *Lodge and house on the hill above*

43

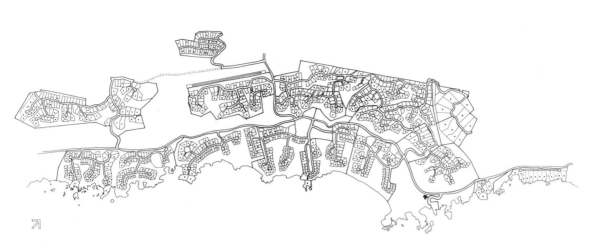

24. *Composite map of the Sea Ranch*

25. *Houses in the meadow*

26. *Houses in the meadow*

harder by a desire for early profit, has been concerned more with salable images of suburbia than with the preservation of the lonely meadows of the past. (24)

But that house on the hill! It is pea green and flares out beyond its foundation, lurching over the grass it shadows. It is hard to classify its relation to the land: it isn't merging with anything or surrounding anything, or enfronting anything. It seems to be at once claiming the land and kicking it. These hills seem large at first, but how vulnerable they turn out to be, and how easily they are destroyed. And how ill-armed the design committee must be if its "restrictions" can't stop this!

The next surprises come at the first meadow, where the Esherick houses are. These have weathered in seven years, and although some of the sod roofs have lost their grass, others have gained wildflowers and the whole group has come to seem an inevitable part of the landscape, as "natural" (and yet as much formed by the hand of man) as the hedgerows themselves. They fit so well because they respond so precisely to the landscape that they add to it, as the hedgerows do. They have not been regimented, like soldiers lined up for inspection. They respect their circumstances individually, but in concert, and with the kind of agreement about intentions akin to that at Edgartown or Santa Barbara.

Across this same meadow, however, the early planning decisions have not been so fully vindicated. (25) A row of houses crowds forward, away from the hedgerows, to see beyond present or future neighbors to the ocean. They stand so far from the trees that they lose their protection from the wind, and they also lose the chance to look like a part of the hedgerow. They seem, too, to be attending to the rhythms of altogether disparate drummers.

Three shed-roofed houses in another corner of the meadow look rather like the Esherick group, but where the sheds of the Esherick houses all faced the same way, into the prevailing northwest wind, the roofs of these houses face in different directions, in response to the lot lines or to some other consideration of the drawing board rather than to those of the place.

Farther north along the coast the confusion of purpose is even more apparent. (26) Here, on more recently developed land, the hedgerows are farther apart, and the wide meadows more crisscrossed with rows of house sites. A remarkably consistent building idiom has developed, partly, one supposes, from examples already set and partly from the pressures of the restrictions and the architectural committee. Vertical redwood board siding and shingled shed roofs create an apparent consistency of style, but show no evidence of agreement about purpose. And the relations between the houses, or between the houses and landscape, is no more apparent than the order of the dots on the salesmen's map that show which lots have been sold. Even distinguished houses sit aimlessly on the meadow, unsupported by neighboring landscape or building forms.

The efforts to achieve a suburban subjugation of the landscape under lawns and bushes are mercifully few. (27) The most popular reaction to the site is conquest by sheer show, making an object on the land that screams for attention as a shape, and not as a place to live in; the relationship of these houses with the land seems less like partnership and more like rape. (28–29) But even when careful attempts are made to build forms sympathetic to the land, single-family houses are seldom massive enough to seem more than tiny bumps on the landscape. A great virtue of the condominium

27. *House with a suburban lawn*

28. *House in the meadow*

29. *House in the meadow*

format (30) is the possibility for dwellings to come together into a partnership with the land which individually they are too puny to achieve.

This appraisal of the Sea Ranch may seem inappropriately harsh; it certainly is tinged with disappointment. Let us first note that in many ways the Sea Ranch *is* a successful place, fun to be in, and much of the magic of the site is still there. But let us also admit that with each new building the magic is diminished a little. What went wrong?

For one thing, most of the decisions were not made on the spot, and this is often characteristic of our times. Even at the beginning, when Al Boeke and others were often on the site, important choices were made in Honolulu by accountants with an eye on the cash flow, and by a board of directors deeply concerned with macadamia nuts. And since the Sea Ranch is mainly a second-home community, people and their architects met elsewhere to develop together their fantasies, quite independent of the spirit of the place. Those same media-driven winds which blew the "Sea Ranch idiom" abroad and made it famous also blew uncaring versions of Swiss chalets and split-levels to this splendid brooding coast. With the owners of the land in Hawaii and the buyers in San Francisco, the salesmen, having only a transient interest in the place, forced a premature packaging of homesites for quick and easy sale.

But we guessed wrong, too, we who planned together to make this place special. We sought a partnership of buildings with this vast landscape which required more size and presence than most houses have, and more care in the arrangements than most people working somewhere else chose to give. In Edgartown, centuries of concern show directly. In the more instant Santa

30. Old condominium

Barbara, many houses merge, behind high hedges and walls, and leave the theme-making to a relatively few buildings of public orientation and distinction. At the Sea Ranch, houses merge into the forest with great success; in the meadows, however, houses need to set up partnerships with the land forms and with each other which turned out to be very difficult to achieve. Most of the houses on the meadow or the grassy slope are reduced to laying claim to their patch of turf. These houses are the least successful, and having said that, we have in all honesty to admit that it is in this way that most people build houses every-where—one by one, without any relationship to each other. What, then, are the chances for a person who wants a good house, and what, in the late twentieth century, is the place of houses?

The place of houses

Edgartown, Santa Barbara, and the Sea Ranch show some of the ways in which houses contribute to the creation of a memorable place. Whole communities which have succeeded, or at least tried for success, they give a sense of what the place of houses can be, and show, in a parade of examples, that no one way, no level of low art, or high art, or middle art has a monopoly on the principles of building.

Our theory of the place of houses, advanced here as a pragmatic device to help you decide what decisions to make, has to begin from a single point of view. To our minds the legitimate purpose of architecture, to lay special claim to parts of the world ("insides") and to set them off from the rest ("outsides"), has turned about on us. We have overbuilt, and often built so badly that instead of having what, for instance, the Middle Ages had (where most of what was built was secure and everything outside the walls scary), we have now made a world in which the most alien things are what we have built for ourselves, while nature by contrast looks good.

What we have built does scare us. Most of it has no message for us. We can't claim it as our own, and we can't comfortably inhabit it. Thus the legitimate search for roots has become frantic, as people seek to anchor themselves in an increasingly bland and undifferentiated geography.

The failure of our surroundings to establish where and who we are seems to us to require a search for the *habitable*—both the physically habitable, where we can be comfortable and live our lives, and the metaphorically habitable, where we can go beyond where we actually are to wherever our imaginations will transport us. Establishing a territory for habitation, physical and metaphorical, is the prime basis of architecture, and therefore of house-building and of this book.

So far we have tried to show two things:

A house is in delicate balance with its surroundings, and they with it.

A good house is a created thing made of many parts economically and meaningfully assembled. It speaks not just of the materials from which it is made, but of the intangible rhythms, spirits, and dreams of people's lives. Its site is only a tiny piece of the real world, yet this place is made to seem like an entire world. In its parts it accommodates important human activities, yet in sum it expresses an attitude toward life.

Ours

We looked at three places because we like them and because they show what we like. They demonstrate, encouragingly, that houses built in concert, and with care, make towns where it is a great pleasure to be. But they indicate, too, how increasingly difficult it is to find that area of human agreement which allows houses to be built in concert. For the individual householder, indeed, the town is generally a given. Some people, ready to make a house, already have a parcel of land, so the neighbors and the outlook are a given, too. Still others have an existing house or apartment, so that the very walls are given. All this sets tight limits on the opportunity for concert with others and enlarges the importance of care in staking out one's own environment, in a new house or a remodeled one or even in an apartment, where special claim can be staked out only with furniture, color, and light.

These limits are not cause for discouragement or despair. Indeed, we believe that building, or remodeling, or simply furnishing a house can provide immensely satisfying returns. The following houses from our own work represent what can be done when the owners are willing to make that extra investment of energy and care. They are new houses because that is what our practice included. They were built in the early sixties and are, as it happens, mostly quite modest and mostly freestanding. Having other clients would have led us to produce other results. The one compelling similarity of these examples is that they are individual, special both to people and to a place.

In our practice we have held to the belief that houses must be special places within places, separately the center of the world for their inhabitants, yet carefully related to the larger place in which they belong. We have ourselves had a set of predilections, including a passionate interest in buildings of the past and a special fondness for barns, which have a way of exhibiting with candor the practical needs and the specific decisions that determined their shapes. We have also admired buildings, like those in Santa Barbara, that display with equal candor the dreams and pretensions of their owners.

Many of our clients have had small and

inelastic budgets, but most of them have been able to boast splendid, or picturesque, or at least challenging sites. Some of the houses have been for vacations, which increased our freedom to interpret people's life-styles in the experimental realm of vacation living. Because of this special freedom, we have been able to regard the smaller houses, especially, as single stages on which many dramas could be played.

The houses are best described in their own terms, but a preliminary word about our formal ideas is in order. We believe the image of "house" holds great power over the human mind, and that a house should seem the most important place in the world for its inhabitants. From the earliest times, four posts, generally surrounding a hearth, have marked this spiritual center. In the huts of primitive man, this four-posted hearth was surrounded by nooks devoted to the storage or use of specific implements. Later the four-poster, with a roof added, became the symbolic house, the aedicula, in which, for instance, pharaohs were crowned, and later still, altars or statues of saints were enshrined. (1–2)

In our own work, the aedicula provided a way of accommodating this general need for a symbolic center in the midst of the specific demands of the household. (3)

Another way has been to build a simple room, an unencumbered central space, and to drape around it spaces for specific use, like so many saddlebags. (4) In larger houses there may be several general spaces, and they may include an outdoor court or a passage. (5)

One of our first house clients was the family of Cyril Jobson, an advertising man from the San Francisco peninsula, who had bought land in a canyon near the coast below Monterey. A road follows the bottom of this canyon, paralleled by a small stream.

1. Ciborium from the church of Santo Stefano, near Fiano Romano, Italy, twelfth century, now in the Cloisters, New York

2. Baldachino, Chiesa degli Scalzi, Venice, by Baldassare Longhena, 1649

51

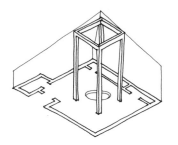

3. An aedicula

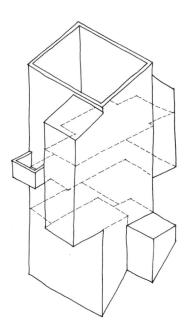

4. Rooms added like saddlebags

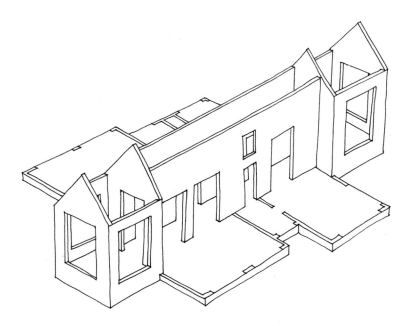

5. Rooms arranged around a passage

Across the stream, a narrow ledge had been bulldozed; beyond it, to the north, rose an almost vertical slope covered with redwoods. Light was therefore at a premium under the trees, and money (hence space) was at a premium in the cabin. This meant that sleeping accommodations, though they were required for parents, grandparents, three children, and their friends, had to be compact so that as much space as possible could be allotted for doing things together.

This was our first aedicular house. In its midst stands a latter-day aedicula, a four-post frame surrounded on three sides at the second-floor level by a mezzanine, and topped by a giant sloping window which affords a view of the redwood trees on the south rim of the canyon. (6) A stair up the center to the mezzanine replaces the hearth of the primitive model. We fancied that it was a celebration of a young family in constant motion. Around the frame, a shingled roof slopes down in every direction—"like a giant redwood tent," noted Frei Otto, a famous maker of real tents. (7) Where the roof has not far to span, as at the mezzanine, the space enclosed is narrow and high enough for two stories. When the roof is allowed to extend farther, as over the dining area, a single-story space with a high ceiling is formed. (8) When it extends farther still, as over the living area, the space becomes even lower, and more intimate. In one place the roof slopes so far that it barely clears the glass doors onto a deck over the stream. (9)

The shapes of the windows are specific to the views they frame and the shape of the walls in which they are cut. The low, wide windows in the living area disclose a gentle view of hills up the canyon; the high, narrow window in the dining area looks onto a spiky young redwood; the glass in the doors is set low to disclose decks one can

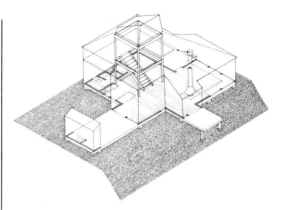

6. Jobson house, Palo Colorado Canyon, California, by MLTW, 1961

7. Exterior, Jobson house

53

8. *Dining area, Jobson house*

9. Outside deck seen from the stairway, Jobson house

10. Living area, Jobson house

walk out onto, and in the corner of the living area a special low, horizontal pane of glass allows an intimate view of the stream below. (10)

The house was built of local redwood in the style of a small barn. The roof framing, exposed and very thin, displays the simplicity of the structure, whose beams span from the center to the perimeter walls. The lightness, the visibility, and the simplicity of the posts and rafters invite you to share vicariously in the act of building.

Our other way of organizing houses is perhaps even simpler than providing a central aedicula. It starts with a simple room, empty and waiting for human action, with specific provisions—kitchen, bath, storage, and the like—appended in little sheds hung, like saddlebags, onto the central space. These sheds are cheap, and they give the houses kinship with the California barns that we and our clients admired.

The first saddlebag house was built for Marilyn Bonham, a young woman who taught school in Berkeley. Her parents had given her a part of their property in the Santa Cruz Mountains below San Francisco, a hillside shadowed by monumental stands of redwood trees, ordered in Druidic circles around the burned-out trunks of still older redwoods. The house was to be used mostly for parties and weekends; the building budget was $7,500, tiny even in 1961. (11)

As it turned out, a huge window netted with steel mullions (our cheapest alternative then, wildly expensive now) enfronts the redwood forest. (12) Behind it the single, unencumbered room struggles to be big enough for it and makes up in height what it lacks in area. (13) The room, in fact, is only fourteen feet square, not really large enough for much furniture, so slight changes in level—up to an entry and window seat and down to an adjoining hearthside—

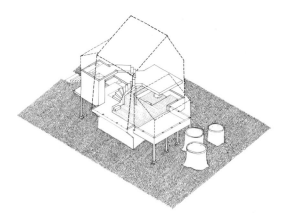

11. Bonham house, Santa Cruz County, California, by MLTW, 1961

13. Living area, Bonham house

12. Exterior, Bonham house

14. Living area and stairs, Bonham house

15. Living area and porch, Bonham house

16. Exterior, Bonham house

provide places to sit and put things, and reduce the vertical distance required to get to a bedroom loft, so that a short stairway, the most there was room for in the tiny space, might suffice. (14) Beyond the bedroom loft, more stairs lead to a bathroom hung in a saddlebag which also contains the entrance and kitchen below. On the other side is a screened porch which extends the room past a huge sliding door which can be pushed out of the way when the weather is fine. (15)

Since there was little room for furniture inside, we used color to make the whole interior into furniture: an orange fireplace inglenook, a blue bedroom rail, and a purple stairway stand out against the white walls. And we were, by our own admission, reveling in the very cheapness of the cabin: plywood walls, industrial windows, exposed framing, tar-paper roof with wood battens, and a cheap metal chimney flue. (16)

The house, though tiny and economical, possesses great apparent size. A kind of dream grandeur comes from the constant juxtaposition of the spacious and the close: oversized windows and undersized stairs, a tight sleeping balcony floating in space, the central room clasped at its sides by roughly built shacks, all of it set among the redwoods on a diminutive foundation and a curious array of posts.

In the Talbert house, in Oakland California, the central room is stretched vertically and fitted out with balconies so that the space can be sensed (though not seen all at once) snaking down past them. Front and rear, at the appropriate levels, saddlebag lean-tos hold kitchen and bath, balconies, and a bay for sitting. (17)

The client, a professor of astronomy, who was a bachelor then (he was later married in the bay window), came to us in 1962 with a lot sloping down from the street at

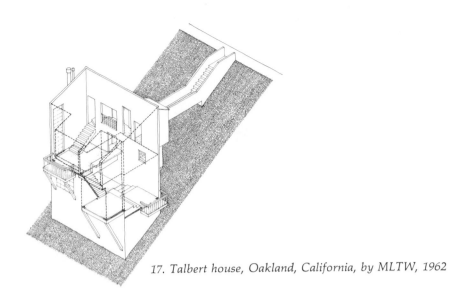

17. *Talbert house, Oakland, California, by MLTW, 1962*

18. *Exterior, Talbert house*

19. *Living and dining areas, Talbert house*

a rate just short of the alarming 60 percent that would render the site unusable. To minimize foundations—the pouring of which involved a rope around the builders' waists and other Alpine devices—a slim tower was decided on. (18) Access to it had to be from a garage at street level.

We felt strongly that a house over a dramatically steep slope, with a splendid view, should capture inside some of the kinetic excitement of the site, and not just be a flat-floored ranch house on stilts. To that end, the entrance is at the top of the house, where one crosses a bridge and enters a foyer that is still outside the main tower walls. From there movement is organized in a descending spiral as you pass by a bedroom balcony and descend behind the wall to the other end of the main space, where an open-railed stair breaks through the wall and down to the dining platform. A few steps lead down from this to the projecting glassy bay, and a series of broad platforms and steps wind on down to end the spiral in the low-ceilinged, close-fitting den. (19) The pace of movement corresponds to the specifics of use, constricted and swift at the top, loose and improvisatory before coming to rest at the bottom. Surfaces within are white-painted plasterboard and dark-stained wood. Windows are small-panel factory sash of stock size, except where sliding glass panels open wide to the view or the decks. The exterior is sheathed in painted plywood, striated more frequently on the appended lean-tos than on the main walls of the tower. These walls are both the literal and figurative structure for the place, for they create a multilevel stage, while the machinery that supports the drama is relegated to the saddlebags. The one exception to this relegation was the furnace, which we developed in the tower as a big black piece of sculpture, whose branching ducts might recall a tree. It recalled no tree to Mr. Talbert, who finally removed it.

Charles Moore's house in Orinda, California (20), provided a chance to tighten the architects' disciplines of formal geometry and to explore ways in which we could accommodate eccentric living patterns a little more daringly than in our houses for others. Here the awesome responsibility of spending other people's money was replaced with the much more relaxed opportunity of spending one's own, all $11,000 of it. There would be no outcry, only rue, over the experiments that failed.

The site was bought one day on impulse simply because it seemed full of magic. It lies in one of the valleys behind San Francisco Bay where the summer sun is warm, on a slope covered with live oak trees. Years before, a bulldozer had cut a flat circular building site, which had since grown grassy and now seemed part of the natural setting, like those perfectly circular meadows that inspired medieval Chinese poets to meditate upon perfection.

The functional problems were simple enough: provision for a bachelor owner who had rigorously excluded from his list of requirements all those things that were not demonstrably necessary. Some of these exclusions turned out to be the work of the devil. It was reasoned, for instance, that a heating system which would always be comfortable at floor level was really only necessary if small children, who were not expected, would be crawling about. Therefore, to save money for more exciting uses, and to induce a sense of being outdoors on the magic site, heating was limited to a small industrial unit blowing warm air down from the rafters. It turned out that most guests regard a sense of being outdoors on the cold ground as undesirable when the temperature dips below freezing.

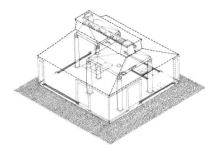

20. Moore house, Orinda, California, by Charles Moore, 1961

21. Exterior, Moore house, Orinda

One opportunity that was especially welcome was for the extensive application of layers of mythic recollection. Tall wooden columns from an old factory were used to ensure that something in this small structure would be grand. The overall design for the house took the archetypal form of a square hut, not unlike those to be found in primitive villages or those symbolized in the motifs carved in the stone of Mayan or Hindu temples. (21) Inside, eight of the columns form two aediculas of different sizes, with unsymmetrical pyramidal covers nestled into the top of the main roof and sharing its large, flat skylight. The vaults of the aediculas are white inside, while the main roof's underside is made of exposed rafters, stained dark and dimly skylit.

The roof is supported by a conspiracy of elements, each inadequate for the task alone. It springs from a ring of beams on top of the outside walls, is caught up by some of the columns of the aediculas, then, under the skylight, a multiple truss—painted orange—in turn serves to hold the whole structure together and to support the rafters that are not supporting it. All that reaches the ground plane are the eight columns, the exterior walls (which never come to the corner), and a layer just inside the exterior wall for shelves, cooking machines, and a water closet. The beds are grouped around a giant bookshelf in the space between the pavilions. (22) The furniture groupings are free to take their places in changing patterns under and around the larger pavilion. One exception is the smaller aedicula, which enshrines an oversized sunken bath and shower, a celebration of the act of bathing here liberated from the cramped conventional bathroom. (23)

Light enters the house in three ways: from the corners where sliding barn doors, mostly made of glass, open to the oak

22. *Living and sleeping areas, Moore house, Orinda*

23. *Bath, Moore house, Orinda*

woods; from a skylight above the truss through which it filters into the larger space, and from the same skylight through the white-surfaced vaults of the aediculas. While the light in the pavilions is not much brighter than the rest, it is dramatically defined and reinforces the structure of the place—the sense that there are many places to go within a single large room. You can be under a vault, or next to a column, or away from the pavilions and wander loosely within the larger, barnlike space. On the other hand, the distinction between indoors and out is at once sharp and manipulable. The large sliding barn doors allow the corners to be either closed or opened entirely to the outside. But when they are open, there is not an imperceptible merging of inside and out, rather the excitement of a boundary that can be leaned out over. This plunges the piano, at the edge of the forest, into a kind of exhilarating jeopardy. (24)

The house has been enriched by collections. The columns themselves, lovingly scraped, washed, and painted at their capitals, are objects to be enjoyed in their own right as well as to be incorporated in the structure of the place. Many smaller objects tucked between the layers of the outside wall serve as reminders of the care with which others, too, have made things in the past.

When Charles Moore moved to New Haven the chance to do all this came again. There the problem was, in a sense, the opposite: a small dark house built in the 1860s and distinguished mostly by looking very much like the drawings of a house made in first grade. It was on a tiny lot on a dark street near the Yale campus and needed some kind of inner explosion if its owner, with his California-based sense of ample space, were not to suffer claustro-

24. Corner of living area, Moore house, Orinda

phobic fits. There was no point in gutting it; it would still be very tiny. The solution, finally, was to gouge out portions of the inside and to insert two-story shafts, giant cabinets filled only with space. (25) The first shaft, named Howard, starts by the entry door and drops to the reclaimed basement (26); a second, called Berengaria, rises midway through the house, reaching from the first floor through the second and the attic to a skylight at the roof; a third, Ethel, drops from a lower skylit shed roof at the rear to the kitchen in the basement below. (27)

Each of these towers is made of double-layered plywood walls with large geometric cutouts that play against each other, emphasizing what depth they have and suggesting much more. The shapes of the cutouts, especially in Howard, are meant to set the mind going to complete the geometric patterns they start, letting it, for instance, extend an arc to a full circle too large to fit in the tiny house. These shafts don't hold anything besides space; they are much more comfortable for humans to be next to than to be in. But they do serve to expose and enliven the house, to lead the mind beyond it and thus loose its claustrophobic grip. They lead your eyes down into its depths, up into the attic, or along a path of associations toward Rome. Stairs beside each shaft allow the body to follow the mind's eye (at least to the attic), plunging directly from the entry to the lower floor, twisting around Berengaria to the second-floor bedroom, bath, and sauna, or easing down broad steps toward the garden at the rear with its panoramic vista of the adjacent Holiday Inn, then doubling swiftly back beside Ethel to the protection of the kitchen. (28)

Surrounded on all sides by alien turf, the house develops vistas and dimensions

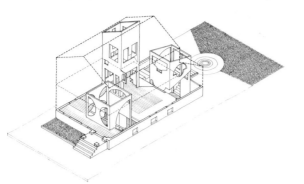

25. Moore house, New Haven, Connecticut, by Charles Moore, 1967

27. Ethel, Moore house, New Haven

26. Howard, Moore house, New Haven

28. Ethel, Moore house, New Haven

internally. Photographs, drawings, statues, favored objects, and especially toys inhabit the recesses of its layered and interweaving walls at every available scale, peopling the house with recollection and fantasy to enlarge the illusion of the place.

In an altogether different kind of setting, in Healdsburg, California, another fantasy, of the forest, is developed more quietly with rooms which open up to allow the whole house to become a great screened porch, a pavilion sitting among the trees.

The house was built for a San Francisco lawyer, his wife, and their children for weekends and summers in a beautiful oak forest overlooking a pond on the family ranch seventy miles north of San Francisco. In those hills, the summer is six months long and almost cloudless; during that time, when the house is generally used, rain is virtually unknown, the days are hot and still, and in the evening cool breezes blow.

In that nostalgic world of quiet summer days, a very simple house, like the classical farmhouses of California or Japan, seemed in order. (29) The California farmhouse of memory is a gabled or hip-roof rectangle surrounded by porches which keep off the hot summer sun. In our version, the walls themselves are made so they fold up against the porch ceiling to merge rooms and porch inside and out. (30) In each corner lies a room, two bedrooms in opposite corners (31), and in the alternate spaces a kitchen and a living room. (32) The living room corner breaks the system: its walls of fixed glass and glass sliding doors reach to the edge of the house and give it space and outlook even in winter, when the counterbalanced walls in the other rooms are shut down against the wind and cold. (33) The living room has a cozy fireplace for those winter days and nights.

For the closed-up winter days, and the

29. Budge house, Healdsburg, California, by MLTW/Moore–Turnbull, 1966

30. Kitchen, Budge house

31. Bedroom, Budge house

32. Living room, Budge house

33. Kitchen with walls down, Budge house

34. Center space, Budge house

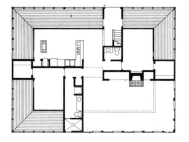

35. Plan, Budge house

summer too, the middle of the house, unlike a classical California farmhouse (but like a California barn), is open inside to the peak of the roof, where skylights dramatize a center for the house. A stair leads to the nearer half of the upper floor; its more distant half can be reached only across a drawbridge under the skylights. (34)

The organization of the plan is as simple and symmetrical as the encompassing roof suggests it will be. (35) And the journeys into fantasy come not by way of collections of miniature things, as in the house in New Haven, or in aedicular memories, but from the light that filters past the branches of the giant oaks and the errant summer breezes that rustle through their leaves.

We have dwelt at length on houses we ourselves have helped to make in order to show by specific examples what the place of a house can be. The design of a house proceeds from an understanding of the land on which it is to be built, from common agreement about its use and its place in the community, and from the budgets, needs, and most importantly the dreams of the people who will live in it. With so many variables there can of course be no one way of proceeding.

Until very recently, though, twentieth-century architecture has followed a series of rigidly constructed orthodoxies, each usually associated with one great architect's name, and these orthodoxies have given birth to the incorrect notion that there is just one way of approaching any problem at hand, a way deemed correct and readily distinguishable in the zealot's mind from all other ways. There are, after all, a great many ideas that houses can convey, a great many moods they can reflect, and many things they can tell us about the people who care for them. Houses can be grandiloquent or shy, reticent or flamboyant, witty or cynical, or moving or silly or even robustly grotesque—as long as they mean something to the people who live in and around them.

Another notion of orthodox modern architecture which we are anxious to contradict is that eclecticism is the ultimate evil, and that collecting physical details or wistful images from past times or distant places, is deplorable. This scorn is non-sense, and the banishment of eclecticism contrary to human nature. Every house has to be "like" something in order to mean something to its inhabitants and to give them pleasure. Making a house "like" something often involves a process of miniaturization; most of the shapes that continue to have meaning in houses come from buildings or natural forms which started out with cosmic importance, from which they were scaled down, reduced, partially reproduced, or just suggested—miniaturized—so that the archetypal power over the mind of the palace or temple still remains in the little house.

We have shown you some of our houses, with their miniaturizings, their likenesses, and their variety in order to bolster your courage in the face of the awesome proposition of planning your own house with all the no-sayers waiting to tell you you cannot have what you want, or that you shouldn't. You may be intimidated by architects and decorators, gouged by builders, denied choices by developers, and perhaps driven to distraction by just about everybody involved. But if you have confidence in what you really want then your task is simplified into a series of orderly choices.

At the outset there are three distinct realms to be considered. In smiling allegiance to classical precedent we call them the Three Orders: the Order of Rooms, the Order of Machines, and the Order of Dreams. Rooms form the basis of a house; they are the empty stages for human action. Different from these are the machines in a house, which have a very specific purpose. Different from both of these are the dreams that the house embodies, and which make it a special place to be.

The three orders

The order of rooms

In most places, at most times, houses have been made of rooms sized to their purposes and limited by economic resources and the techniques for putting a roof over them. Clusters of activities were assigned to rooms, and the spaces were called living rooms, parlors, dining rooms, bedrooms, and so on. The rooms generally were discrete and could almost always be closed off from each other by doors to assure privacy or to maintain warmth in winter.

In early American houses tradition provided only a few ways of putting rooms together to make a house, and most of these ways resulted in a box. Once the early American housebuilder settled on the number of rooms he needed and the limited number he could afford, the task was to choose the pattern which put them in an appropriate relationship to each other. The process was a model of clarity and simplicity.

These patterns of assembling rooms had often appeared in response to the resources, climate, and topography of a particular region. Later they were transported from one place to the next, so they could be found almost everywhere. The earliest houses in New England, for instance, had small leaded-glass windows not just because that was the style (though the cottages of England certainly provided models) but because glass was expensive, and came in small sizes, and it let in undesirable amounts of winter cold. Arranging rooms around a central chimney, too, conserved heat in the bitter winter. (1)

Farther south in Virginia the winters did not present such a surprise to the early colonists, but the hot summers did. There fireplaces were often put next to the outside walls of the house rather than in the center, so as to arrange the rooms along a central corridor which ran right through the middle and opened to the outdoors at both ends, and was thus better able to attract errant breaths of air. (2)

Farther south still, in Charleston, a town densely built on a small peninsula, the air was apt to be endlessly sultry, and even in the eighteenth century land was fairly scarce. Accordingly, a typical Charleston house faced the long side of its tiny lot, not the narrow street front. In it the rooms lined up in a row and opened onto broad covered porches which ran the whole length

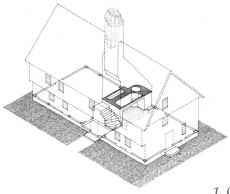

1. Capen house, Topsfield, Massachusetts, 1683

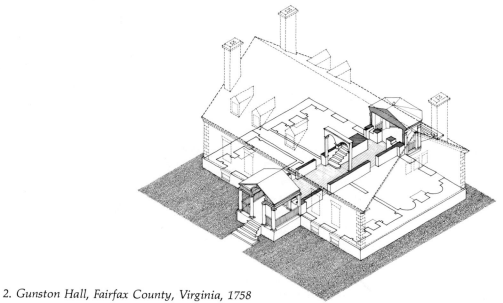

2. Gunston Hall, Fairfax County, Virginia, 1758

of the house, often on both floors, to catch any breeze and at the same time to provide shade. (3)

In the Deep South, where the land was flat and wet and sometimes even flooded, the main rooms of a house were sometimes raised above the ground in a country-style version of the tradition of Italian palaces, whose architects had often raised the major rooms one level onto a *piano nobile* and put spaces on the ground where comfort was deemed less important. Southern plantation houses often incorporated a porch which ran around the whole building, and during the hot months this became the main living place. (4)

The hot and dusty winds of the Southwest demanded an opposite response. Here comfort could be achieved by closing out the dry winds with rooms arranged around a patio, where the green grass or the trickle of a fountain could add to the real as well as the apparent cool. Buildings in the desert needed a heavy material which would keep out the winds and retain the cool of night. Adobe was cheap, fairly durable, and readily available, and so it became a natural choice. (5)

These early houses in New England, Virginia, South Carolina, Louisiana, and the Southwest show that in each region there was a preferred way of assembling rooms to make a house, and this way provided a loose framework of choice for each house-builder. Not everyone followed the preferred mode, but many did, because it struck a convenient balance between what most people needed and the requirements of the location.

The simple processes of wrapping rooms around a solid or an open center (as in the Capen house or the Southwest house), or arranging them on either side of a corridor (as at Gunston Hall), or lining them up in a row (as in the Pringle house), or wrapping them around with a veranda (as at Homeplace Plantation) have all enjoyed an amazing durability. Four of the six possibilities for assembling rooms in your own house are contained in these early regional examples.

Of almost equal durability, but not quite, has been the tradition that rooms must always be discrete and self-contained. By the latter half of the nineteenth century, architects were building houses out of rooms which had begun to lose their traditional separateness. They had become more irregularly shaped and were often linked to each other by large archways and sliding doors. (6)

But it was Frank Lloyd Wright who, more than any architect before him, devised a surprising redefinition of the room. His search for what he called an Organic Architecture led him soon after 1900 to a dissolution of the apparent barriers between one room and the next. What resulted were houses in which the basic unit was still the room, but where, at least in the public areas, the rooms merged subtly and elegantly the one into the other to make what came to be known as an "open" plan. (7)

Just as on the inside he erased the barriers between one room and the next, so on the outside, to use his phrase, Wright "exploded" the old-fashioned box that houses had always been, extending the rooms outward in separate wings so that the shape of the whole house was no longer closed and compact, but flowed out across the land and seemed to merge with it, rather than stand apart. (8)

The Modern Movement in architecture, influenced by Wright's published works, was begun in Europe in the decades after 1910 by men like Walter Gropius, Ludwig Mies van der Rohe, and Charles Edouard

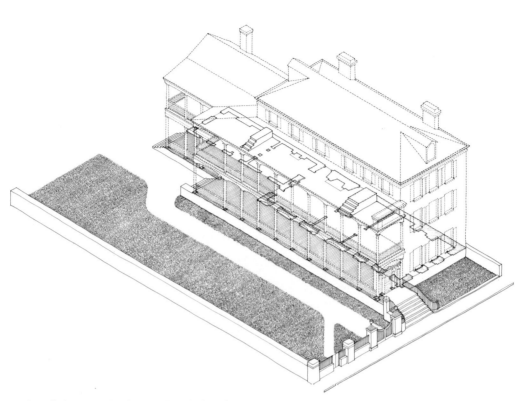

3. Pringle house, Charleston, South Carolina, 1774

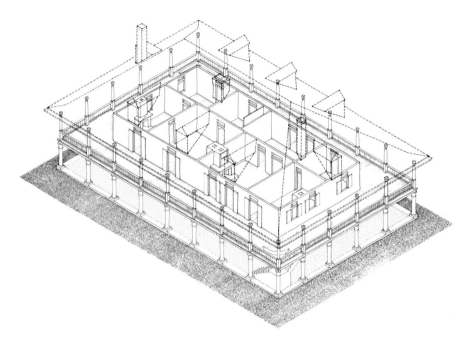

4. Homeplace Plantation, St. Charles Parish, Louisiana, ca. 1801

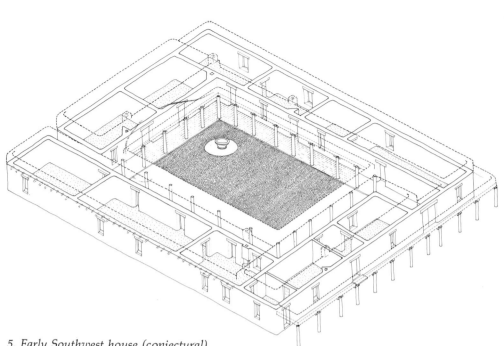

5. *Early Southwest house (conjectural)*

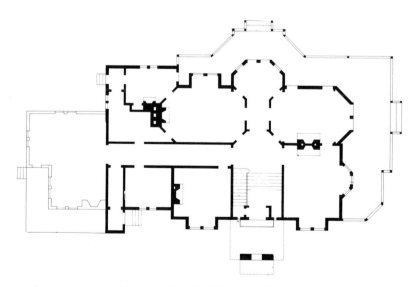

6. *Griswold house Newport, Rhode Island, by Richard Morris Hunt, 1863*

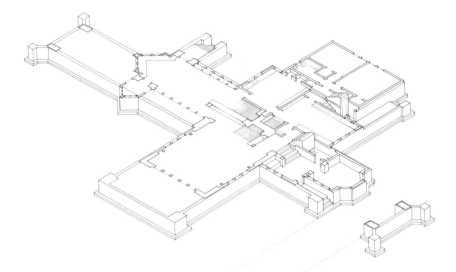

7. Willitts house, Highland Park, Illinois, by Frank Lloyd Wright, 1902

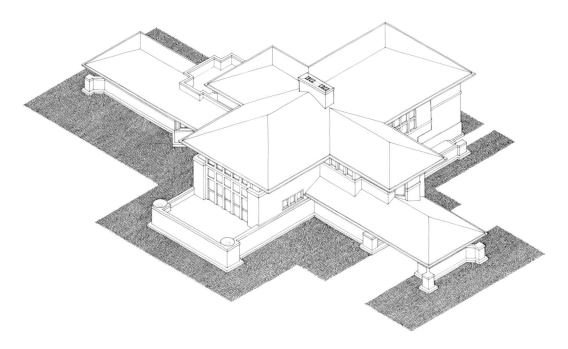

8. Willitts house

Jeanneret-Gris, who called himself "Le Corbusier." These pioneers conducted what must surely be history's most self-consciously revolutionary attempt to change the course of house building, and they rigorously allied themselves not with the traditions of the past, but with images of the present and future. In doing so they carried Wright's redefinition of the room a step further. A project for a house by Mies van der Rohe illustrates one extreme result of their efforts. The house, which was never built, was divided into spatial zones, here by a free-standing wall, there by two walls abutting. It has no discrete rooms, only a single space which slips and slides through the house and even, by an outward extension of the walls, to the outside. There is an abstract, graphic purity in the whole design. (9)

No arrangement could be less like those of our five early-American houses. Yet it illustrates a mode of planning that has dominated Modern architectural theory. We might then ask what brought about such a dramatic new way of putting a house to-gether. New ways of seeing things, provided in part by sleek machine-made materials, give part of the answer. So do the new ways people were living in houses by the first decades of our century. Fewer people could afford to build really spacious houses, and those who could found it harder and finally almost impossible to get servants to keep them up. In addition, a house was becoming less a place for generations to live and more a place where a family would spend only a part of their lives and then move on.

It even began to seem questionable whether certain functions, like daily dining for four, deserved a special room. The smaller number of rooms a family needed and could afford now had to serve a variety of separate activities, and so the shape of each room and its relation to all the others took on a new importance.

The necessity for discrete rooms became less important, too, since central heating improved the chances for keeping warm. In fact, since about the middle of the nine-teenth century all kinds of machines had been gradually added to houses. Today they are regarded as essential components of any house. They control and circulate the air inside, they give light, they cook and pre-serve food, they carry away waste, they clean our bodies with water heated up by other machines, and they use up most of the money in the budget.

The development of the open plan in the twentieth century shows a concern not just for the novel configuration of rooms but also for the problem of accommodating machines. Le Corbusier expressed his generation's preoccupation with the machine in his famous pronouncement that a house is a machine, a machine to live in.

Unfortunately, there is a mundane denoue-ment to the story of the Modern Movement. When we drive through towns and suburbs we notice that not all new houses are "Modern." This is curious because, for instance, in the Georgian or Federal or Greek Revival periods of architectural history, most houses, big and small, looked Georgian, Federal, or Greek Revival. Now every suburb and town has at least one or two "Modern" houses, but they are the exception rather than the rule. Most new houses are "traditional" and look vaguely like "Williamsburg" or "French Provincial," or they are "Ranch Style" and look even more vaguely like the work of Wright. Many are a strange combination of all these things at once.

Possibly this is so because most families are anxious to cultivate images in their houses of their real or imagined ties with

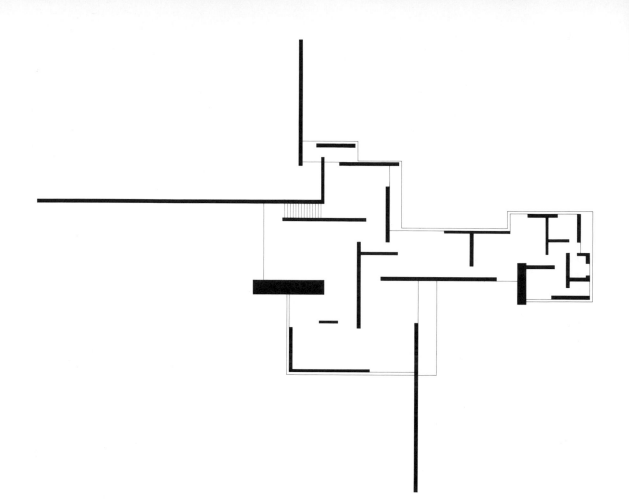

9. Brick country house (project), by Ludwig Mies van der Rohe, 1923

the past, rather than face uprooting visions of the future. It may also be so because the new ways of planning a house proposed by the Modern Movement sometimes ignored the fact that certain areas in a house should at times be separate, and that others must be private. The traditional room, separate and clear, still has its appeal.

In the past most machines were portable, when they existed at all, or, like kitchen machines, were banished to an outbuilding. So when we admire buildings from the past we almost always find ourselves admiring rooms. The rooms juxtaposed formed the houses, and our admiration is sustained by their clarity. The elegance of a Georgian house like Gunston Hall is underlined by the simplicity of its formal arrangement—four beautifully proportioned rooms on the ground floor with a hall passing through the middle. The house is ordered entirely of rooms; kitchen and baths and even closets are not part of the arrangement, and the spatial purity is unsullied. (10)

Most twentieth-century houses are still put together in old-fashioned ways. They begin at least as an assembly of rooms. Then machines are inserted. The result is that spaces once carefully formed for dignified human habitation have been marred by machines. (11) To accommodate the machines we have given up the clear and gracefully proportioned rooms (as well as the icy corridors and chamber pots) of our ancestors' houses. When the provision for machines receives more careful attention than the provision for human habitation the house becomes not a place to live in but a setting for equipment. The result is a house made of a mishmash of rooms and demirooms and nonrooms so bland and disorderly that the only things the owners think to mention in the real estate ads when they seek to unload them are the number of bathrooms and

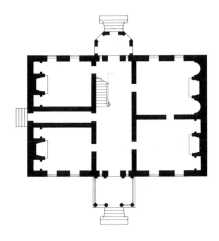

10. Gunston Hall

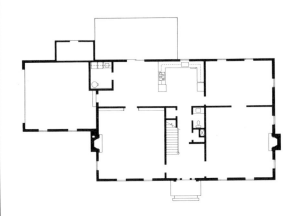

11. A modern "traditional" house

81

kitchen appliances and the source of power for the heating system.

It doesn't have to be that way. The task of making a good house is much more easily understood if rooms are approached *as* rooms, and machines *as* machines.

These distinctions require us to use the ordinary words "room" and "machine" in slightly special ways.

A machine is a piece of domestic equipment which assists us in a *specific* task. Most obviously this includes refrigerators, dishwashers, sinks, stoves, lavatories, tubs, showers, toilets, furnaces, and the lot. Less immediately obvious, but still included in our special nomenclature may be closets, stairs, built-in benches, beds, and shelves, and in fact any fixed object to which we go for help in performing a particular act. It is useful to think of the spaces around machines not as rooms but as *machine domains.* Machines and machine domains exist to serve us in our house, not to dominate, and they serve best when they do not infringe on the more general purpose of rooms.

Rooms are *unspecific spaces*, empty stages for human action, where we perform the rituals and improvisations of living. They provide generalized opportunities for things to happen, and they allow us to do and be what we will. When we understand rooms in these ways, we can address freely their qualities which are hardly ever mentioned in the real estate ads, the essential qualities which give them a memorable sense of being special places to inhabit.

The empty stage of a room is fixed in space by boundaries; it is animated by light, organized by focus, and then liberated by outlook.

Space

Rooms are made of walls, floors, and ceilings, but they seem to be made of space, a commodity more important than any of its boundaries, though created by them.

One horizontal dimension of the space, its width, has always been limited by the techniques for covering it. Through most of history those techniques have been limited to laying simple pieces of stone or wood from wall to wall, or to piling bricks or small stones so they leaned on each other to make an arch, or later, to combining pieces of wood or steel into a truss in order to use the members more efficiently to span larger spaces. Later still, materials like steel with high tensile strength have been used to hang the roof between supporting walls. (12) The visible expression of the act of spanning has been of special interest to builders, and they have sometimes communicated their enthusiasm to inhabitants.

Though architects of public and religious buildings have worked miracles of ingenuity in spanning great spaces, most rooms in houses are sufficiently narrow to be covered over more simply. When the width of a room is small enough, say under twenty-four feet, so that it can be spanned with beams of wood or steel or concrete, then a flat ceiling is normal, though it is by no means required. Simple rooms simply spanned have always given pleasure, and they are not unsatisfying if their ceilings are high enough to avoid any sense of oppression and to make us feel comfortable in our sense that the ceiling will stay well above our heads.

In rooms of great width some configuration, usually by way of making the room higher in the center, is often psychologically desirable, and it also allows people to participate imaginatively in the act of spanning the space. (13)

The other horizontal dimension of rooms,

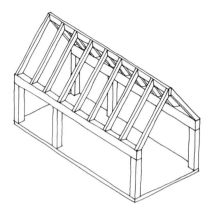

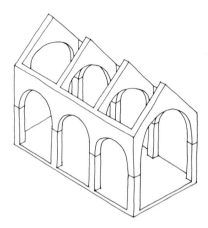

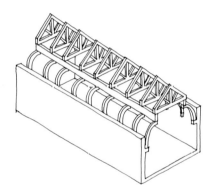

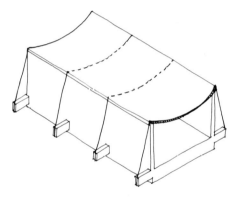

12. *Covering a space*

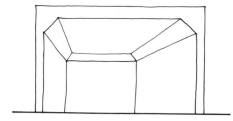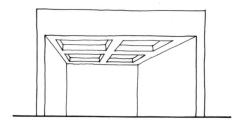

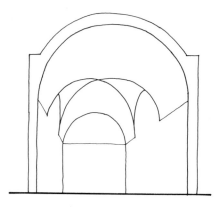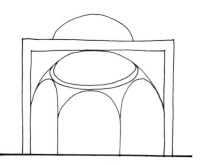

13. *Configuring a ceiling*

their length, is not of course limited by structural necessity, but by means and desire. *Pasajes*, *loggie*, *gallerias*, *galeries*, and English long galleries have traditionally stretched the long dimension of rooms to great distances, inviting movement through them. (14) Most rooms, though, are meant to be places to be *in*, to do something alone or with other people, and a long narrow room may generate an unsettling sense of motion.

A square room acquires a special formality, a static quality that comes from the identity of its length and width. The Great Hall at Stratford, in Westmoreland County, Virginia, has this power. Thirty feet square, and enhanced by the sloping edges of its tray ceiling, it verges on the totemic, with its curiously strong sense of being in the middle of things and unmoving. (15) The architects of English country houses, following the lead of their admired Italian master Andrea Palladio, often exploited this formality in three dimensions and made their great central chambers into perfect cubes.

Most rooms, though, loosen the fixity of the square by being longer than they are wide. Some claim that the Golden Mean, in which the length is about 1.6 times the width, assures the most pleasing shape. In the sixteenth century, Palladio himself gave just seven ways to make beautifully proportioned rooms. (16) Other famous architects have added to the canon additional shapes to which they have attributed special powers over the imagination. (17) Magic aside, we know of admirable rooms which range in shape all the way from round to square to long and narrow. All of the proportional systems which some architects have sworn by, and others sworn against, seem to us to be functions of recall, for they allow the architect systematically to re-create the feeling of some well-admired room or set of

14. *Long Gallery, Syon House, Middlesex, England, by Robert Adam, 1761*

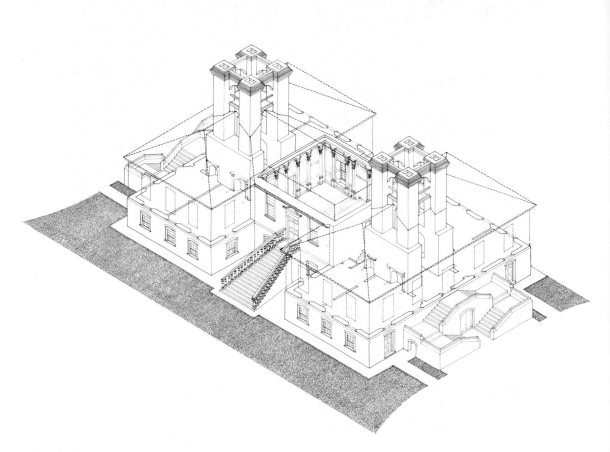

15. Stratford Hall, Westmoreland County, Virginia, 1725

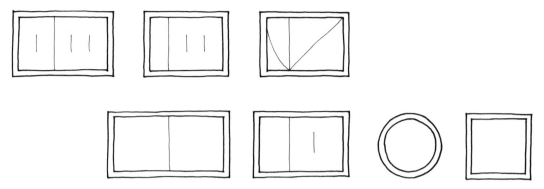

16. Palladio's seven ways of proportioning the plan of a room

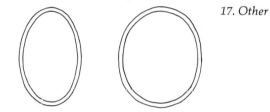

17. Other traditional ways of proportioning the plan of a room

rooms remembered from another time.

Rooms whose length is much more than twice their width often seem to break down into more than one area. (18) Sometimes, of course, this ambiguity is desired, as in the Long Gallery at Syon House, where fireplaces and groups of furniture make pools of quiet along the line of march.

The Lawrence house at the Sea Ranch contains another sort of long room, one that changes from a high, rustic baronial hall at one end to a low-tiered stage, wide open at the other to redwoods, meadows, and miles of coast. (19)

This house was built as a vacation retreat for a recently widowed woman and her three children. She had bought a lot at the edge of the forest, high above the coastal meadows. (20) The long room, which begins with the panoramic view, steps down to the fire place area and kitchen, and in turn opens onto a southern deck at the back of the house. An exterior ramp on the north side leads to the main entrance, next to which a staircase rises over the kitchen to the master bedroom suite. Underneath, on the ground floor, are children's rooms.

It is the main room itself which harbors the spirit of the place. The ceiling and each of the thick walls are surfaced with rough boards which reflect a rich warm color. As these walls reach down to the level where people move and touch things, they are hollowed into shelves and niches for storing objects, then finally smoothed into painted plasterboard surfaces before they touch the shiny wood floor. The master bedroom nested in the top of the main space forms a sheltering ceiling for the kitchen and eating place just below. Its yellow wall reflects sun from a skylight, and an opening at one side allows a view down into the main room, or from below, a surprising glimpse up to trees and sky beyond.

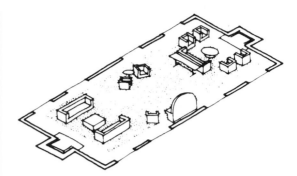

18. A long room organized into several areas

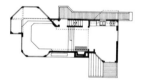

19. (From top) Upper, main, and lower levels of Lawrence house, Sea Ranch, California, by MLTW/Moore–Turnbull, 1966

20. *Exterior, Lawrence house*

21. *Living and dining areas, Lawrence house*

22. *Sitting area, Lawrence house*

An antique high-backed seat in the center of the long room invites repose by the fire and provokes association with the great halls of English manors. (21) At the low-roofed end of the room the space spreads beyond the confining walls into broad, cushioned platforms and enfolding bays formed like nests in the tops of the trees. The steps and platforms invite a casual family gathering. They allow each person freely to pick his position in relation to others sitting close to the ring of conversation or lounging slightly beyond and above it, staring off to the sea. (22)

Length and width, the two horizontal dimensions of rooms, determine the ways in which people are encouraged or even required to move. The third dimension, height, has a power at least as great as the other two dimensions to create the spatial quality of a room.

Through history, architects have put down as many formulas for determining a room's height as they have for describing its length and width. One principle which always obtains is that feelings of loftiness, or of coziness, or simply of comfortable proportion are a function not just of a room's vertical dimension, but of that dimension in relation to its other two, width and length. The standard eight-foot ceiling which architects inveigh against and which builders keep on building has in itself no automatic merits or faults, save the merit that it has been standardized to relative cheapness. In a very small room it can seem surprisingly high; but in a more-than-moderate-size room, eight feet can feel discouragingly low.

Even the impressions of height or lowness, though, do not carry with them positive connotations of grandeur or oppressiveness. Those of us who feel uneasy and betrayed by eight-foot ceilings in many modern houses often warm to the low ceilings in

parts of Frank Lloyd Wright's houses, and to the very low ceilings in old New England houses, where the beams may come less than seven feet above the floor. Possibly we like these spaces because they are unusual and strange, in the former case the product of an architect's deliberate intent, and in the latter the result of a tradition which calls up for us images of far-off, half-forgotten worlds. They do not therefore pose the threat of general blandness that standard builders' houses do.

Small variations in the height of a ceiling seem to have the power of altering the feeling of space much more than the same variations applied to the width and length of rooms. Raising a seven-foot ceiling to nine feet, for example, will produce a striking spatial change, whereas the change between an eleven- by fourteen-foot room and one twelve feet by fifteen feet will not be so noticeable. One explanation for this is, of course, the fact that in most rooms the vertical dimension is considerably less than either of the horizontal ones, and so small changes in it are more noticeable than the same changes applied to the plan. But it also seems true that the vertical dimensions of rooms, since they are relatively free from "functional" imperatives, are able to carry more than their share of emotional content.

Variations in the feeling of height from one space to the next in a house provide useful opportunities for variety and surprise, and for giving the inhabitants a sense of where they are in each instance and of how that place is different from all the other places in the house.

In some older houses we admire, the separateness of the rooms is underlined by the fact that to get from one to the other one must pass through a low door which penetrates a thick wall. The doorway is a partial vestibule, a mini-room, small and

23. Doorway from an eighteenth-century house

low, which marks the passage from one habitable space to another. (23) The technique implicit here can be exploited more variously. The transition from a generously proportioned bedroom to a low adjoining bath or from an expansive living area to a cozy study can reinforce the sense of different activities for which each space is intended. Similarly, the act of arrival and penetration of the house can be celebrated by the surprising juxtaposition of a low vestibule or entrance portico with a high stair hall. (24)

The exploration of spatial variety, as well as the departures from simple traditional shapes is not uncommon now, and there are many reasons for it. The primary one is that since rooms are empty stages for human drama, and since human drama contains elements of ritual and of improvisation, rooms are bound to reflect the relative importance of each. In a time like ours when ritual seems to wither and improvisation flowers, the shapes of rooms are likely to become more casual. Our technology provides some other reasons. Spanning spaces grows easier, and walls of glass make indistinct the limits of our rooms. Changing circumstances figure, too. Once a series of rooms accommodated a series of uses— dining, studying, sleeping, entertaining, and what was vaguely called living—allowing for distinctions among rituals and providing a variety of backgrounds for improvisation. Now, since space itself costs more and more, we act out our complicated lives in what may be no more than a single room, and so we are likely to require of that room a dizzying versatility.

The Ottosen house in Junction City, Oregon, is fundamentally one room under a large sloping roof high on one side and head height on the other. (25) At midpoint the roof is supported by two sets of large,

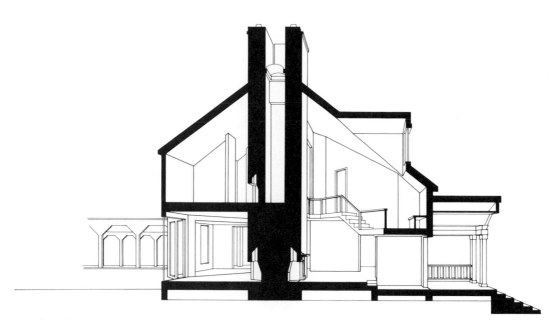

24. Smyth house (project), by Gerald Allen, 1972

25. Ottosen house, Junction City, Oregon, by MLTW/Lyndon, 1967

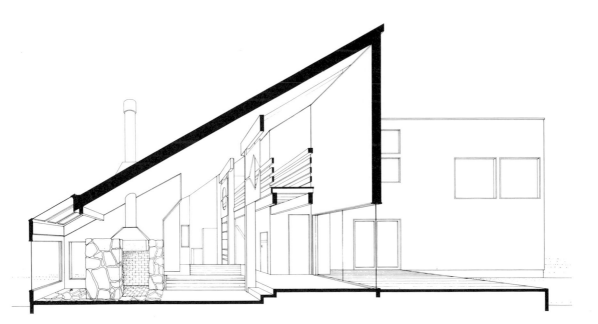

26. Section perspective, Ottosen house

rough-cut columns and thick beams salvaged from a neighboring barn. The room is a simple one, with cooking space at the entry end, dining space in the middle, and conversation and sleeping areas at the opposite end. (26–27)

The configuration of the roof, its supporting structure, and the sleeping balcony that runs along its high side differentiate many locations in the room. At the entry and kitchen end the roof bends on the diagonal and is cut into to make space for an entry porch and a window which lights the stair inside. The cooking area is a cul-de-sac. In the middle of the room the outside wall steps in to make room for a sheltered eating porch under the roof's eave, while skylights just inside the wall brighten the dining area within. Next to the dining area and a few steps down is a large stone fireplace pulled close to the eave; behind it the roof line continues lower still under glass into a tiny solarium beyond the eave, dug into the earth and facing the flat fields beyond. The edge of the roof, low at the fireplace, extends up and across the room along a smooth, white, diagonal wall sparked midway by a small skylight. At the far high end of the room is a fully glassed bay facing a cluster of trees. The balcony stops short of this end of the room so that the high space can be filled with light. (28)

There are places that are bright, dark, sheltered, high, close fitting, and far reaching, all within the confines of the single room. The room is enlivened, principally, by exploiting the slope of the roof and the structure that holds it and introducing light in various ways through and around it.

27. Interior, Ottosen house

28. Interior, Ottosen house

Light

The room, limited by shape, is animated by light. Traditionally rooms in houses have not always had a great deal of light because other concerns—the need for heat and privacy, as well as the cost of glass—have militated against it, and custom has often decreed the use of screens, venetian blinds, curtains, and draperies to control and at the same time minimize what little light small windows gave. The natural light source in a room, nevertheless, has great evocative power, and the image, for instance, of light falling through shutters onto polished floors, or illuminating the sides of deep-set windows, or sliding across a white wall, as in the rooms Vermeer painted, strongly color our remembrance of places. (29–31) What we mostly remember, of course, is not the light source itself, but the surfaces onto which the light falls: the polished floor, the casements, the wall. The Cary house near San Francisco, by Joseph Esherick, was one of the first houses we know of to ignore the competing styles of the early twentieth century, which required either walls of glass ("Modern") or small holes poked in walls ("traditional"). Here window openings are used to provide for needs beyond the utilitarian. Light falls once on a wall, once on a floor, and from one window into nothing, since it is there to provide outlook; and these openings combined establish the mood of the place. (32)

Light, as it enters rooms, has variations of the most compelling sort. The directions from which it comes are critical. Human eyes hurt when they are confronted with great contrasts of light and dark. A room whose light comes in from one side only will be filled with glare, the objects and people within it will throw disconcerting shadows, and if it is dark enough inside, and bright enough outside, the eyes' effort

29. Russell house, Charleston, South Carolina

30. Orangerie, The Queen's House, Greenwich, England, by Inigo Jones, 1616

96

31. The Music Lesson, *by Jan Vermeer, 1660*

32. Cary house, Mill Valley, California, by
Joseph Esherick, 1963

to adapt will cause some pain. If, however, the main source is balanced with light from the other direction (33), from above (34), or even from a side wall (35), far greater comfort will result.

A surface reflecting light, like the white walls in Vermeer's room or a light floor or ceiling (36–37) can spread and at the same time soften the light source. Even a daylit surface around a window inside or outside can provide a surface of intermediate brightness, softer than the sky outside, but far brighter than the interior wall on which no daylight shines, and this mediation itself soothes the eye. (38–39)

The qualities of light—soft, sharp, pellucid, or crystalline—stay vividly in our minds. Daily variations, too, condition our impression of rooms—the bright sunniness of a morning room, the cool dark of shuttered bedrooms, the shadowless bright of the artist's studio. All these qualities of light we can predict, within the limits of geography and the local climate, and plan for, since for any location the sun follows a known trajectory through the sky. Natural light, changing during every hour of every day and varying with the weather and the seasons, makes a room come alive.

Artificial light, however artful, is a necessary but necessarily limited extension of it. The shifting qualities of natural light, keeping us connected with the natural processes of the earth and with time, have in their infinite variety not yet been approximated with artificial light. Though our electronic capacities certainly would allow us to program artificial lighting arrangements changing over time and in quality ("Martha, put on the afternoon in Marrakech, with the thunderstorm") the absence of any real connection with the natural world, and all that means to us, would still be marked. Artificial light, however fanciful its source,

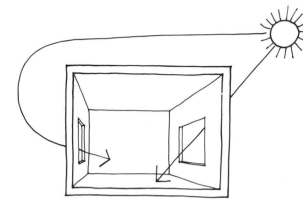

33. Light balanced from both sides

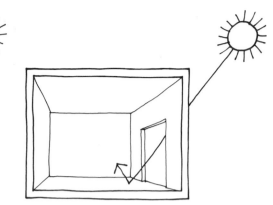

36. Light reflected off a floor

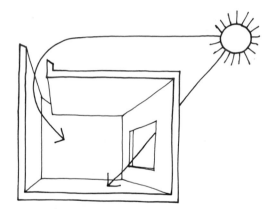

34. Light balanced by a skylight

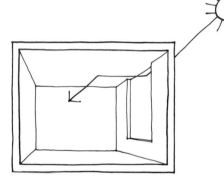

37. Light reflected off a ceiling

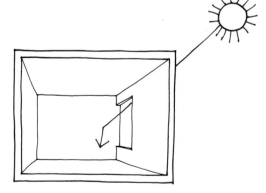

35. Light reflected off a wall

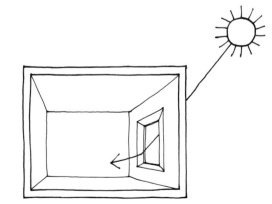

38. Light reflected off the side of a deep-set opening

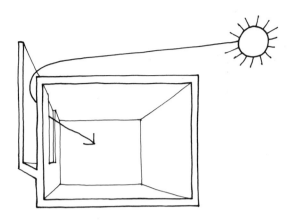

39. Light reflected from a wall outside

usually remains constant over time, and offers few surprises.

Focus

Another major and critical characteristic of rooms is their provision for movement and repose. Repose is encouraged by a single focus, which collects attention, organizing the room around a center of interest, like a fireplace or a couch or even around itself, as in the square hall at Stratford. Most of the Georgian rooms we admire focus on a fireplace, decorated with the care which befits its importance, an importance which used to include the comfort of the fire's warmth, as well as the fascination of its flames.

The designers of Japanese houses, with their characteristic subtlety, raise to a high art the provision of a focus in the *tokonoma*, a niche where a favored picture and perhaps some flowers in a vase are placed. These objects reinforce the emotional content of ritualized actions like the tea ceremony which takes place in front of them. (40)

Our own focuses are rather more casual. Some, like television sets, are meant to transport us, and so have a focal importance out of proportion to their size. Perhaps the most interesting are those meant, like the *tokonoma* itself or like any collection, to provide a clue to the owner's sensibilities. (41) We require that the clues to our host's concerns be combined and multiplied and personalized. A coffee table laden with the objects its owner derives pleasure from and which reflect his current concerns serves a useful role, enhancing verbal intercourse instead of killing it as the television does.

As a single focus induces repose, so multiple focuses induce movement of the body itself or of the eye. The open gallery in the Santa Barbara Court House is measured by a long series of arches, multiple

40. A tokonoma

41. Pyramid, Moore house, Centerbrook, Connecticut, by Charles Moore, 1973

focuses which animate an empty stage for moving. The Long Gallery at Syon House, as we have already seen, offers both multiple and single focuses.

Our Stern house depends, too, on moving focuses to induce movement of the body and the eye along two axes at acute angles to one another. (42) The plan is based on two long galleries, one real and one partly imagined. Each one runs the full length of the long house, and the two cross at the center, where the house becomes very thin and glassy and open to terraces north and south.

The first gallery, sometimes narrow, sometimes wide enough to be used as a room, begins at the front door, from which one can see over a hundred feet to the living room at the far end of the house. (43) Proceeding down this gallery, one can shortly look out to the right over the lower family room, then on the left the hall opens into the dining room. Further along, the space opens up above and to the right to accommodate a stair and to allow a view of the intersecting gallery, bridging above on the second floor. At the crossing of the paths two routes become evident, uniting beyond the stairs to form the living room. (44)

From the crossing, a diagonal look backward would have disclosed another axis, past the family room to the garage. Above it, on the balcony, lies the other long gallery, under a sloping roof where windows, evenly spaced, but stepping up with the eave rather than maintaining a constant height above the floor, induce a dimension of change to the act of walking along the space. At both levels, but especially at the lower, the points of termination, and of rest, come not separately, but from a swelling of the spaces along or at the ends of the lines of movement. Living area, dining area, the family

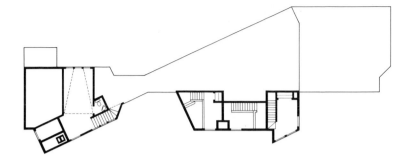

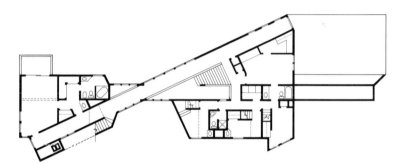

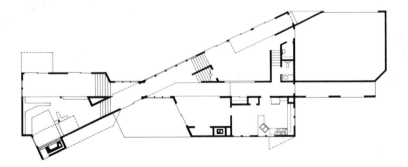

*42. (From top) Upper, middle, and main levels, Stern House,
Woodbridge, Connecticut, by Charles Moore Associates, 1970*

43. *Interior, Stern house*

44. *Interior, Stern house*

room, all stay or arrest the galleries' lines of motion. So the main spaces of the house are stretched out in passages inhabited by people moving. If you see a corridor as nonroom, as wasted space, then this house is wasteful. If you see it as a room stretched, an empty stage for moving as well as resting, then here are rich chances for improvisation.

In a far smaller house, the Jobson house described in "Ours," the moving focus is vertical, or at least it is a sloping one, a stairway which attracts the participant and rewards him with a view of redwoods out the high window at the top. It attracts as well the imagination of the viewer, since stairs are so clearly a symbol of motion upwards, so that a focus moving vertically stirs the space, and extends it.

Outlook

Focus organizes the space inside rooms. Of equal power is outlook, in which something outside the room attracts the attention of the inhabitant without requiring him to give up those advantages enclosure brings. Outlook occurs through openings, generally windows, and is, in effect, another kind of focus.

The power of outlook is enhanced if some elements in the foreground, like the window itself, serve as a bridge between the near and the distant. A balcony or a deck or some nearby planting can also extend the foreground and frame the view.

In Japanese gardens careful distinctions are made between foreground, middle ground, and background, with particular attention to getting the most out of the outlook, forcing the foreground closer and making the background recede, elaborating the sense of almost infinite vistas even in tiny city courtyards. (45) Often these vistas exist by themselves in nature, and the only artfulness required is that of placing a

45. *A small Japanese garden*

46. Picture room, Soane house, London, by Sir John Soane, 1824

window so that they can be seen from the inside.

The effect of outlook, at its simplest, is not unlike that of a picture on the wall, except that views of the outside world are animated by changes in the weather and the seasons and often have elements which move even as they are being viewed. Paintings can provide artificial substitutes. In the rear of Sir John Soane's house in London there is a tiny room which would open to a rather dismal courtyard on one side and a not very pretty street on the other. Instead of windows there are pictures, not just one on each wall but dozens, ingeniously hung on hinged panels that open in succeeding layers to provide the viewer with a long series of artful outlooks. (46)

Rather differently, a small entrance hall in Charles Moore's house in Centerbrook, Connecticut, opens on one side to a tiny courtyard constrained at the back by the concrete-block wall of an adjacent factory building. Here a painted-on window copied very loosely from one by the seventeenth-century architect Giulio Romano, and incongruously hung with a double-sash window, provides a surprising outlook to an otherwise drab vista. (47) The effect is more improbable than absurd—improbable that this window should be just inside a doorway in rural Connecticut, improbable that the whole thing, so simply painted, seems as real as the sliding glass door in front of it.

Bay windows, porches, and solaria take outlook one step further, allowing the inhabitant to move outside the enclosure of the room. (48)

One contemporary phenomenon, explicable only in terms of the urge for exposure rather than outlook, is the ubiquitous suburban picture window. Architects who had used large windows or windowwalls to dramatize the virtues of outlook noticed

47. *Courtyard, Moore house, Centerbrook, Connecticut, by Gerald Allen, 1970*

48. *Bay window in the Faculty Club, University of California at Santa Barbara, by MLTW/Moore–Turnbull, 1961*

49. A token tokonoma

some time ago that most suburban picture windows faced the street where there was no privacy and no view. They scoffed at an idea misunderstood. But it is likely that what they scorned was another idea altogether, the idea of exposure, not outlook, in which objects (like lamps with ruffled shades) were meant to describe the inhabitants' concerns and were exposed to the gaze of passersby, like an outward-facing *tokonoma*. A passing car, however, provides less chance for contemplation than the tea-ceremony room. (49)

The drama can be public or private, enjoyed by many or by one alone. But it is fulfilled in spaces that are formed and focused by human care. Space, light, focus, outlook—and, especially, the care for all those—are the qualities which make real rooms.

The order of machines

Machines in a house, as we have rather specially defined them, can be divided into two groups: those which are self-operating and those which require people to operate or use them. In the first group are furnaces, air-conditioners, and water heaters, machines which once adjusted perform their services nearly by themselves and need attention from us only for occasional maintenance, or when they break down. In the second group are machines which we confront directly. They assist us in a multitude of ways, helping us perform specific and often regular domestic activities.

Machines, whether they are self-operating or need us to run them, require spaces. These are, in our terms, "machine domains," not rooms. This terminology frees us from the stereotypical notions, which do not always hold, that a furnace must be put in a furnace room, that a stove, sink, and refrigerator must be in a kitchen, or that a toilet and a shower must be in a bathroom.

There are only a few general rules for locating self-regulating machines in a house, and almost none of them are sacred. Air-cooled central air-conditioning units, the kind many houses will use, have to be placed outside, somewhere where the noise and heat they generate will not be a nuisance to the inhabitants or the neighbors. Furnaces, for the greatest efficiency, can be put near the center of the house, and water heaters, in allegiance to the same goal, should be put near the taps they serve. It is of course not easy in some cases to put a furnace near the center of the house, and it can usually, with only a little loss in efficiency, be put in almost any accessible place, generally beneath the floor. Similarly, it is sometimes not easy to locate a water heater near all the taps it serves, and in the case where one heater serves two taps at opposite ends of the house, it is impossible. In this case you must decide whether you can tolerate hot water taps which take minutes to warm up, or whether you can afford two water heaters or a circulating system, or whether you should relocate one of your sinks.

The two most common types of heating systems are hot water and warm air. The first pumps hot water, or occasionally steam, to individual radiators throughout the house. The second supplies warm air, which is heated up at the central furnace and blown into the individual room through ducts. Central air conditioning is provided also by ducts through which cool air is pushed from a single source, and so when air conditioning is required a warm-air heating system is frequently used to avoid the necessity of two separate circulation systems.

Most people prefer to have furnaces, air-conditioning units, and water heaters, as well as the ducts and pipes connected to them, somewhere out of sight. With a modicum of foreplanning, ducts and pipes can be fitted into the wall cavities and the floors and ceilings of a house. Waste pipes, since they work by gravity, must be fitted in with a bit more care. If, for example, they serve fixtures on an upper floor, there must be sufficient space between that floor and the ceiling below it for the pipes to be slanted enough to drain without interfering with the structural members of the house.

There is another alternative to all this. The pipes and ducts do not have to be concealed at all, but can be left completely exposed, like beams and trusses in a roof, to suggest the kinetic processes that make the building work. They can also serve, less solemnly, as the basis for decorative inflection and fantasy. (1) When they are left exposed, though, they may have to be made more carefully and more neatly than is customary when they are concealed, and this extra tidiness may add extra expense.

Of all the rubrics for mechanical equipment in a house the most familiar is the one which dictates that bathroom fixtures and kitchen sinks be put back to back when they are on the same floor and above and below each other when they are on different floors. This, one is told, saves money on the plumbing, which is generally true. But the savings are not always as great as one is led to believe. A plumbing system is, of course, an expensive item in the total budget of a house; but a greater percentage of its cost goes for fixtures and fittings, and expecially for the labor required to make them, than for the lines of pipe themselves. Thus if it seems supremely desirable to have two bathrooms, each at opposite ends of the house, it can usually be done without ruinous expense.

There are nevertheless good reasons for clustering sinks, baths, and toilets in a house, though the reasons are as much conceptual as economic. Doing so can be a useful discipline for ordering these machines and their domains so that they do not impinge on the separate and nonspecific spaces in the house, the rooms. Clustering, of course, is not absolutely required, but if the spreading of baths and sinks and toilets all around the house betrays a set of random and casual decisions, then it is suspect.

Machines like furnaces, central air-conditioning units, and water heaters, and also their ducts and pipes, are rather easily disposed of in a house simply because we do not have to approach them very often. Their domain is their own, not ours. The accommodation of operated machines—stoves, refrigerators, dishwashers, tubs, showers, and the rest—is more difficult because they all need us in some degree to make them work. Their domain is ours, for our sensibilities presumably do not change when we leave our living spaces and approach them in their special domains.

These machines assist us in specific activities like cleaning, storing, and preparing food and washing and purging our bodies. Devices like closets, stairs, beds, and benches, which are less literally mechanical, but which for our purposes we regard as machines, also assist us in storing away our clothes and other possessions,

1. Exposed duct in a house in Boston, Massachusetts, remodeled by Hardy, Holzman and Pfeiffer, 1968

moving up and down to different levels, and supporting our bodies in long- and short-term repose.

The sizes of beds are determined by the dimensions of the human body and by our preference, at least in Western cultures, for resting on a soft and resilient surface, like feathers or foam. In our society bed sizes are fixed, and these are given, together with the sizes and shapes of the other standard components of a house, in the section headed "Yours."

The domains around beds are susceptible to more variety than the beds themselves, since they are determined entirely by human predilection. Mrs. George Washington Vanderbilt's bed at Biltmore House, in the mountains of North Carolina, is, in our special terms, a richly embellished machine, serving one specific function in a place consecrated to a host of unspecific improvisations. (2) Set on a dais and hung with a canopy of purple velvet, it provides the focus for the large room. A large bay window on the opposite wall provides light and outlook to the Blue Ridge Mountains on the horizon. This dais is a machine domain; the rest is a room in which many unspecific activities can take place.

In the remodeled bedroom of a small two-room apartment in New Haven the bed is a one-piece, multipurpose machine designed to sit in the middle of a tiny space and serve from various sides the activities of sleeping, dressing, working at a desk, and storing away books, papers, and clothes. (3) Here the domains for all these specific daily activities are of necessity shared in one small space, made to seem more generous than it is by large windows cut in the walls. These separate the different machine domains and allow views, for instance, from the desk into the rest of the room and to the one beyond. What began as a rather bland

2. *Mrs. Vanderbilt's bedroom, Biltmore House, Asheville, North Carolina, by Richard Morris Hunt, 1895*

3. Bedroom machine, New Haven, Connecticut, by Gerald Allen, 1971

room—with at least the qualities of space and light and a modest outlook over a parking lot, softened in summer by a willow tree—ended up primarily as a machine domain, no longer a room, once the multiple machine had been added. There was little opportunity left for quietly talking, or casually moving about, and these activities migrated to the other, less tightly configured room in the apartment.

The disposition of beds and their domains can impart a wealth of connotation to these basically simple machines, be they rich or utilitarian, formal or casual. Fewer implications are usually attached to clothes closets, which should merely keep clothes available for when they are needed, and unwrinkled and out of sight when not. It is this presumption, at least, which has caused us now almost universally to favor built-in clothes closets, a practice which was virtually unknown a century ago. An alternative to this, which may sometimes be attractive, is to do as our ancestors did and hang our clothes in moveable pieces of furniture, which themselves are often objects of great beauty.

Ladders, companion ways, steep stairs, shallow stairs, and ramps, all are devices which make it possible for us to move from one level of a house to another. Their mechanical trick is the Archimedean one of letting us do in a series of small movements over a period of time what we could not do all at once. Steep stairs are tiring not because it takes more energy to climb them, but because the energy is expended over a shorter period of time.

Stairs have always been one of the most fascinating elements of architecture; with their connotations of ceremony and choreography, their appeal is universal, whether we are moving along them or gazing at them from above or below. Worthy of note here are the implications of the decisions whether or not to have vertical movement in a house, and if so, whether it will be celebrated with a large and striking set of stairs, or woven into the fabric of the rooms, or even slipped in almost unnoticed.

Architects have for centuries been moved by the virtues of all these courses. The Nathaniel Russell house in Charleston, South Carolina has a central hall three stories high, through which an elegant stairway sweeps up in a graceful ellipse. (4) On each floor all the rooms open onto the stair hall and onto this most beautiful of stairways. Note, however, what a large area on each floor is taken up by the stairs (5); it was such expenditures that Thomas Jefferson had in mind when he declared that grand stairways inside were wasters of space, and banished his at Monticello, a house considerably larger than the Russell house, to positions of little importance. (6)

Nowadays the space-consuming aspect of stairways is of critical importance to the housebuilder; so is the expense of building a really elaborate stair. It is therefore often common now to treat stairways with the utmost efficiency, forgetting the richness that they can give to a house. It is still possible, however, to include an elaborate stairway in your house, without undue expense, if you are careful to let the space it partly occupies serve other functions as well. Even the stairway itself can serve as a place for sitting or talking, as well as moving.

Our Tatum beach house sports a stairway which becomes not only the main path of motion, but the main space and the very heart of this little vacation house. (7) The stair, a humble version of the sort one would find in a baroque palace, has flights at opposite ends of the space up to a landing at the second-floor level, then

4. Stair hall, Russell house, Charleston, South Carolina, 1809

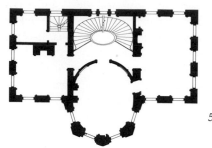

5. Plan, Russell house

6. Plan, Monticello, Albemarle County, Virginia, by Thomas Jefferson, 1770–1808

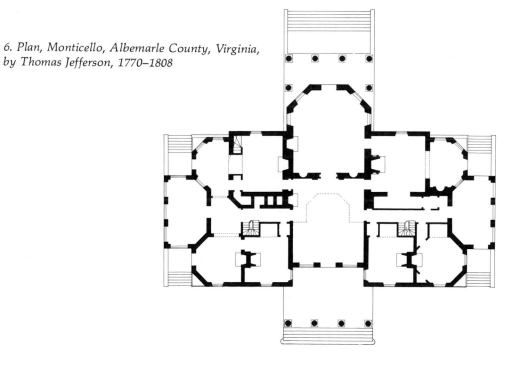

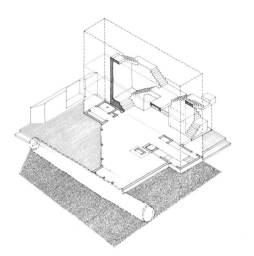

7. Tatum house, Santa Cruz County, California, by MLTW/Moore–Turnbull, 1971

double flights again up to separate bunk rooms for boys and girls. Shelves for books and objects line the space and are rendered accessible by the numerous flights of stairs.(8)

The ceiling is translucent plastic, and the whole effect teeters between shanty and grandiosity. Jefferson would object, and there is an undeniable absurdity to this baroque gesture wrapped in corrugated plastic, but the stairs become, in this little house, a really grand stage for motion and an adept foil for the sitting space, which occupies the other side of the house and opens to the water. (9) The spine of the house, which lies alongside the stair, holds kitchen and dining room at ground level, and two bunk rooms and a bath at each of two upper levels, tight machine domains with openings into the lean-to saddlebags beside the spine. (10)

Everyone is concerned with the machines used to store and prepare food, and a welter of possibilities present themselves for your consideration. There are refrigerators, icemakers, freezers, ovens for baking and broiling, burners for frying, steaming, poaching, and boiling, sinks for washing, and, sometimes, dishwashers. As well, there are smaller handy devices like blenders, mixers, toasters, choppers, and can openers, garbage disposers and compactors. Most people prefer, logically enough, to have all these machines clustered together and, with them, a generous expanse of countertop for working, and even more generous cabinets for storing.

The location of cooking machinery has developed in an ironically cyclical pattern during the history of houses. In older dwellings like the Parson Capen house, the cooking equipment is right in one of the main rooms (page 73). In later, and grander houses, cooking was done in a special room.

115

8. Stair hall, Tatum house

9. *Living room, Tatum house*

10. *Exterior, Tatum house*

a kitchen, sometimes operated by servants and separated from the main house, where it posed less threat of conflagration. Later still, the kitchen was reattached to the house. Only in this century did it become, with any frequency, a part of the main living space once again, as in some houses formed in the "open" plan, and as in the small apartments in which many Americans now live.

The exact location of cooking appliances in your house will depend on a series of questions which you must answer for yourself on the basis of your own tastes, and it will depend on whether or not you will have others to help you as you use them. In the likely event that you will not, you must choose whether you prefer to be alone in a separate place when you cook, or within sight and shouting distance of your family and guests. Or you may decide that though you enjoy their community, you would prefer more strongly not to have your cooking done near or adjacent to the place where your family and guests are likely to be. All these decisions will, as well, be qualified by whether you enjoy *haute cuisine*, or hamburgers, or both, and therefore by the amount of special equipment your culinary style requires.

There have been a number of time-and-motion studies made which can, if you think their message is important to you, be of use in arranging the machines you need. Most of them come to surprisingly negative conclusions about the efficiency with which kitchens are usually laid out. In evaluating these studies and the versions of them that appear from time to time in the popular house magazines and do-it-yourself books, you should decide whether or not it *matters* to you that you should, for greatest efficiency, be sitting, not standing, in front of your sink, or that as you

move from refrigerator to chopping block to oven you are using your small muscles most and your big ones least. Above all, you must decide whether or not you *want* to be most efficient every time you use your kitchen, for that can imply using it the same way, always moving in the same patterns, denying, for instance, the opportunity for intimate friends to nestle into the kitchen during the cocktail hour.

Bathroom fixtures, and the activities that take place around and in them, have also been studied in minute detail by the experts, who have almost to a man concluded that these machines, like those in the kitchen, are from any sanely analytical point of view absurd. Most of us, though, are stuck with them, for better or worse, and can express our individuality and preferences only in the composition of their domains. Many people have noted that the bathroom, as it is standardly built in most American houses, is a conflation of two rather different realms of activity. For the one there is a machine which serves the activity of eliminating, the toilet, and for the other there are machines which we get into to wash our whole bodies (showers and tubs) or stand in front of or sit on to clean only a part (sinks and bidets).

If the act of cramming all these machines into the same room is offensive to you, as it might well be, then you can, for instance, separate the toilet from the tub and sink, as is customary in Europe; you can make the entrance to your bedroom pass through a part of the bathroom; and you can even place the tub not six feet from your bed. Le Corbusier did all these things in the Villa Savoye. (11) One enters the master bedroom through a narrow tiled corridor with a row of closets along one side; to the left of the entrance, but screened from it, is an area containing the sink and a bidet. The toilet is in a separate closet opening into this area,

11. Chaise longue *separating bath and bedroom, Villa Savoye, Poissy-sur-Seine, France,*
by Le Corbusier, 1931

12. *Baths of Diocletian, Rome, ca. 300, reconstruction by Edmond Paulin*

13. *Swim Club, Sea Ranch, California, by MLTW, 1966*

but hidden from the view of the entrance. Between the sink and the bedroom itself and behind the row of closets is the bath, screened from the bedroom by only a shower curtain and a *chaise longue.*

There is usually a ruinous set of inconsistencies built into the stereotypical grouping of three fixtures for these uses into one room, five feet by seven feet, or longer or wider if the funds are ampler. The toilet in many civilizations, including our own, is generally regarded as something meant to be used in private. Army lore, for example, is full of tales of extended periods of constipation in military personnel caused by the characteristically public grouping of these facilities. Washing, on the other hand, and bathing, have through much of the world's history been regarded not only as activities that can be shared without shame, but even as excuses for relaxed social interaction, and for special architectural effect. (12) The whole act of taking off one's clothes, so as to be especially conscious of one's body and its unencumbered movements, and then relaxing, soothed in a series of monumental spaces—all heightened that sense of being somewhere.

Our own best example of a place where bathing can be enjoyed is, probably not surprisingly, where it can be done communally, in the first Swim Club at the Sea Ranch. (13) Its space is tiny, inside some lean-tos between the buttresses of a high wall which serves as a kind of wind-dam, keeping the prevailing breezes off the swimming pool and tennis court otherwise shielded by berms of earth.

Inside the men's locker room, brightly lighted through a translucent roof, the awareness of one's own body that comes from taking clothes off and getting wet (in the shower) or hot (in the sauna upstairs) is reinforced by a simple choreography. One leaves shoes at the floor level, clothes on the first wooden platform; inundation comes two steps above that, in the shower on the right, then dry heat in the sauna, higher up still. (14) All this happens within the vivid movement of shapes and colors against walls of strong white. The details (mail boxes for lockers, infra-red bulbs for heat) are cheap, so not at all like the opulence of Roman baths, but the dance, we hope, is as moving, the unencumbered motion of the body as strongly felt.

Japanese and Turkish baths and Finnish saunas have more consistently preserved to our time the pleasures of the bath. They stand in strong contrast to the American assumption that washing is best achieved by standing on the slippery bottom of a bathtub in a room used chiefly for defecation, your lower limbs entangled in a slimy curtain pulled toward you by the rush of cold air occasioned by the squirt of hot water onto a small portion of your back.

We do not, of course, demand that you change your bathing habits, unless you want to. We do suggest, though, that you consider what you want, free from stereotype. The five- by seven-foot three-piece-package bathroom is surely one of the most evident stereotypes we live with.

Of all the operated machines which assist us the automobile presents perhaps the most puzzling case. It is something less than a room, and considerably more than a machine. It is as well a notorious purveyor of dreams. One would require blinders when looking at modern houses in America in order not to take into account the numerous ways in which, for most of us, the automobile is an adjunct of, and sometimes even a substitute for, a house. For one thing, it constitutes a significant proportion of the space which most of us control. Many automobiles are bigger than the small rooms

14. Men's locker room, Swim Club

in our houses, and the standard provision for a single parking space (200 square feet) is larger than the minimum size of two bedrooms as specified by the Federal Housing Authority. Add to that the area which must be kept smooth and clear for the car's movement from the road into a garage, and you can easily see how consuming of space and resources an automobile is.

As advertising agencies long ago discovered, the stylish automobile is linked to our understanding and dreams of ourselves in much the same way that houses are. Though the Cadillac under the *porte cochère* has recently been supplanted in our magazines by a Mustang overlooking the sea from a rocky shoreline, the automobile still promises to do what a house might have done, to make possible a fulfilling pattern of living. That the promise held out to everyone leads more often to a suburban cul-de-sac than to stately mansions, more often to Jones Beach than to a grassy windswept shore, only underlines the fact that the emblems of distinction, if that is what you want, cannot usually be bought prepackaged, but are more successfully assembled with care by you alone.

A house, of course, can be an important emblem of distinction, or of anything else you choose, if it is developed with personal intensity. The automobile, as a domain which moves, also serves as a packet of personal space that accompanies us. Its dominance over public transportation in cities surely has as much to do with its ability to protect and insulate people as with its touted convenience. The small, faintly luxurious chamber, cluttered with tobacco, papers, and hairpins, sometimes with a coffee cup or perhaps a patron saint, and filled with stereophonic sound is a haven of security from which to assess the passing surroundings, be they beckoning or indifferent.

Several generations have learned, too, to make still more intimate use of the automobile. For many young people, caught between a family they wish to outgrow and institutions they cannot control, it is the only space truly their own, their sole capital investment, the object of their ingenuity and care, and the scene of some of their most private encounters.

The machines connected with a house—be they the curious automobile, or the self-operating machines, or the ones which need us to use them—all can be designed or put together or bought in ways that vary from the conventional to the surprising, the humble to the grand. Even though the possibilities for splendor and novelty are great in the Order of Machines, one can rarely afford to make each one dazzlingly special, nor will most people care to. The task, then, is to choose those, if indeed there are any, that seem to you worthy of particular care, to make these and their domains splendid in the ways which will please you, and to treat the others with dispatch, making sure that they do not spoil the more general stages for living, the rooms themselves.

The order of dreams

The ordering of rooms can provide a context for daily action, and arranging the machines in an orderly way can ennoble specific acts. But still another realm of concern is necessary to make a good house. The dreams which accompany all human actions should be nurtured by the places in which people live.

Houses have always embodied aspirations, and often they have recalled for their inhabitants places and times not quite their own. We have seen striking examples of this phenomenon in Edgartown, Oak Bluffs, and Santa Barbara. It can also be seen, dimly, in the mindless decor of contemporary tract houses and apartments.

Domestic architecture has been a parade of fancies, some sober and economical, some flamboyant. The earliest builder's guides in America reflected a prudent taste for fashionable English models. These manuals were published to assist the Colonial builder in making the details of his structure; they assured that such features as moldings and trim pieces, doors, windows, and mantelpieces could be well made and "correct." Later guides began to provide a broader range of choices, showing, for example, the influence of French architecture, whose virtues Thomas Jefferson extolled. Then the range expanded as more books, travel, and a taste for greater variety increased the store of images to emulate. Sophisticated European publications which reported archeological finds and exotic travels caused the guides to cater to the tastes of the Greek Revival, advocating the ambitious application of whole temple fronts, not just isolated classical moldings or sculptural accents, to houses and public buildings.

Around 1850 the range of available choices widened further, as more people began to realize that there was a greater variety of things that their home could be "like." The pattern books which grew popular around the middle of the century, and effectively put the older builder's guides out of business, helped to bring about this change. They offered the housebuilder a variety of styles to choose from—Swiss and Gothic, Tudor and Tuscan—all rendered with an American accent. Unlike the builder's guides, pattern books gave many plans and elevations and perspectives of whole houses, and they paid little attention to the details. The homeowner was now encouraged to decide whether his dreams would best be fulfilled only by the semblance of arcadian temples, or by rustic chalets or farmhouses. (1-2)

The most famous pattern books were written by Andrew Jackson Downing, a landscape gardener turned architectural entrepreneur. A portion of his thesis was that Greek Revival architecture was bad. He frowned on symmetry and deplored white woodwork, which, he thought, stood out too strongly against the landscape. Downing's arguments over whether a house should be like a classical temple or a rural villa have, or course, long since faded from currency. Nonetheless, he and the older craftsmen, though they disagreed on the particulars, all assumed something which we are inclined to forget—that without question a house should be *like* something.

Late in the century the popularity of pattern books declined. Their demise was in large part brought about by the increasing variety of images they had originally purveyed. By about 1900 the alternatives had multiplied until no book for the layman could presume to be complete. By then there were architects ready to design houses individually, and the profession of architecture had emerged.

Before, almost every architect in America had been either a gentleman amateur like Thomas Jefferson, or a particularly talented craftsman, or a formally trained foreigner. In 1868 the first architecture school in America opened at the Massachusetts Institute of Technology and was soon followed by other schools, so that by 1900 there were men trained in a sophisticated repertoire of the styles of past civilizations, eager to apply them to houses and public

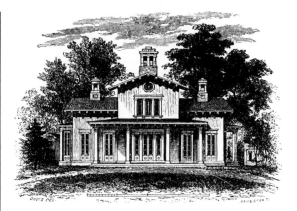

1. *A small classical villa*, from The Architecture of Country Houses, *by Andrew Jackson Downing, 1848*

2. *An Italian villa, from* The Architecture of Country Houses

3. A park lodge, from Rural Residences, *by John Papworth, 1818*

4. A cottage orné, from Rural Residences

buildings. This development coincided with the accumulation of great wealth by a number of families who sprang from humble beginnings and who adopted a lavish lifestyle with a haste sufficiently unseemly to give pundits the pleasure of dubbing theirs the Gilded Age.

Western architecture became a catalogue to be rummaged through, selected from, and aped. The armaments for the legendary Battle of the Styles were thus assembled. The combatants were architects championing Louis XIV, Etruscan, Queen Anne, Romanesque, or whatever; it is not clear whether their clients should be seen in the roles of munitions makers, escalating the war with their money and demands for preeminence, or simply as unfortunate civilian casualties.

The impulse to recall the architecture of the past, though, was not silly. On the whole, people who made their houses recall far-flung historical precedents must have done so because these precedents meant something to them. What they needed, however, was a house, not a Greek temple or a medieval lodge, and so they wrenched the scale and changed the functions of their antique models and wound up with something which was without a doubt their own. Once they had identified what their dreams were, the borrowed framework of whatever style they chose provided a way for fitting together all the pieces. (3-4)

From 1890 to 1895, for instance, Richard Morris Hunt, a most distinguished warrior in the Battle of the Styles, made Biltmore House near Asheville, North Carolina, for a man who wanted to have the grandest country house in America, and who fortunately could pay for it. Hunt chose to build the house in the manner of a French château. It may have seemed a queer choice for the mountains of North Carolina, but it was supremely suited to the kind of house George Washington Vanderbilt, the happy owner, wanted. And once the decision had been made to build a château a great number of successive choices were therefore defined, and the rest of the course became clear. (5) Henry James, who visited Biltmore in 1905, noted at once the irony, even the absurdity, of building at one fell swoop in America a family seat in the manner of European dynasties. "A thing of the high Rothschild manner," he called it, "the *gageure* of an imperfectly aesthetic young billionaire." But James also saw in the house something more than the dazzling display of wealth, and it is this special element that we ourselves most admire in houses and insist upon. "What was this element but just the affirmation of resources?" James asked. "If large wealth represented some of them, an idea, a fine cluster of ideas, a will, a purpose, a patience, an intelligence, a store of knowledge, immediately workable things, represented the others. What it thus came to, on behalf of this vast parenthetic Carolinian demonstration was that somebody had *cared* enough—and that happily there had been somebody *to* care."

The Order of Dreams demands that you, like Messrs. Vanderbilt and Hunt, open up the full range of your own responses to the world, your own concerns. It demands that you acknowledge and display the pretenses which you harbor, that you imagine your house in the ways your daydreams and memories suggest, and that you envision the special places which might correspond to them. Doing this will not produce a design for your house, but it will bring forth a structure of intent to guide you as you make the practical decisions about the rooms and the machines you will need.

The house that you devise will be especially successful if it brings you in touch with the most fundamental human dreams.

127

5. Biltmore House, Asheville, North Carolina, by Richard Morris Hunt, 1895

C. G. Jung has written about these in describing a home that he built for himself in Switzerland. Jung's house grew slowly from one form to another as he added to it during the course of several years. Through building the house he explored a mythic embodiment of the psychic structure he found within himself, and considered to be common to all men. The house became a cluster of three towers, which Jung identified with properties of consciousness. They incorporated differing conditions of enclosure, outlook, and repose. The rooms were embellished with paintings and inscriptions and opened out onto an enclosed garden completed by a loggia. The garden was occupied by a cubic stone on which Jung himself carved Greek and Latin epigraphs. In each act of building he used spaces (like the tower rooms) and objects (like the stone) that had primitive symbolism; nevertheless he also attended carefully to the erudite traditions of his own studies, as in the inscriptions and paintings. He was especially concerned that his actions be guided by more than practical circumstance. "Inner peace and contentment," he wrote, "depend in large measure upon whether or not the historical family which is inherent in the individual can be harmonized with the ephemeral conditions of the present."

When explaining the house, he writes as though he had been compelled by his unconscious to build it as he did, guided by impulses deeper than those of the conscious will. "I built the house in sections, always following the concrete needs of the moment. It might also be said that I built it in a kind of dream. Only afterwards did I see how all the parts fitted together and that a meaningful form had resulted: a symbol of psychic wholeness."

Even so confident an intrepreter of symbolic meanings found it important to follow the directives of his intuitive attachment to things. Through his caring their meanings were extended and completed. The structure of the house became a symbol for his knowledge of himself. These are processes far more profound than those which nowadays try to reproduce the "dream" of a Georgian house by barely approximating its external appearance. In Jung's house, dreams have been transmuted by his passion, forged into a wholeness of form.

The shapes that a house might take have always been limited in three obvious ways. First is what a person can afford. Second is what materials and skills are available. Third is in the range of things a house might be like—what images were known, and which ones society encouraged a person to emulate. Jung used images in a particularly courageous and modern way. But even in Colonial America, as we have seen, this impulse was felt. For the earliest settlers a tradition of what was to be done had developed from the narrow range of what *could* be done and what shapes and embellishments had meaning for them and for their neighbors. (6-7)

Thomas Jefferson was careful to compose the elements of his house, Monticello, in patterns defined by his scholarly vision of republican dignity. (8) The dome, the entrance porticoes, the terraces and tunneled outbuildings are indicative of totally different social pretensions from the more primordial forms described by Jung. (9) To recall on a mountaintop in Virginia the urbane culture absorbed from his library and his experiences as minister plenipotentiary to France, Jefferson assembled the rooms with discriminating taste. He separated the machines of living in niches, subterranean passages, and outbuildings with a practical ingenuity elegant in itself. (10)

6. Doorway, Williams house, Old Deerfield,
Massachusetts, 1756

7. Drop, Capen house, Topsfield, Massachusetts,
1683

8. Monticello, Albemarle County, Virginia, by Thomas Jefferson, 1770–1808

9. Exterior, Monticello

10. Exterior, Monticello

This skillful combination and juxtaposition of the Order of Rooms and the Order of Machines was used clearly in the service of a dream, that of a patrician social order modeled after the classical democracies.

Henry Mercer, building his own fantasy castle, called Fonthill, drew even more specifically upon recollections of shapes and details in other buildings which he had admired during his travels. (11-12) He incorporated in the house a tower suggestive of a French château, windows based on a Turkish precedent, and a wide array of other elements. These recollections, insufficient in themselves, were so numerous and varied that they enabled Mercer to make a house that is unusually evocative and strange. For Mercer himself each reference was quite specific, recalling for instance a particular afternoon in Salonika. For us the references are less obvious, yet they can summon recollections of our own. (13-15)

The power of this place lies in its integrative eclecticism. As a whole, unlike Biltmore House, it reproduces nothing very precisely. All of the references have been transmuted by Mercer's quite personal view and by his way of building with concrete and tile. Mercer was one of America's first anthropologists, an inveterate collector of things, and the builder and manager of a tile works that produced ceramics of exceptional quality and design that can be found throughout the country and, abundantly, within his own house. Informed by this great array of interests and images, his house has many levels of possible effect and meaning.

Jung's, Jefferson's, and Mercer's houses represent very rare cases of the investment of years of compulsive energy by knowledgeable amateurs. An architect, building all at once, and usually for someone else, is faced with the problem of providing an effective substitute for the wisdom and continuing care which these men could bring to their houses. Most often he depends on formal consistency to give cohesion to the house, hoping that the powers of style will carry the requisite meaning.

Easy travel, books, glossy magazines, films, and television have revealed an almost unlimited array of styles our own houses might embody—exotic ones from far away, bold visions of the present and future which Modern architecture has invented, or nostalgic creations from the past which recall some half-forgotten sentiment.

Conspicuously absent among most of these images are heartfelt, personal convictions about what a house really *should* be like. In the absence of dreams all choices are reduced to pseudochoices, no significant choices at all. Without dreams, the other two forces which delimit choice (what we can afford and what is available) are not, as they should be, challenges that spark the imagination. They are simply the dreary material limits which shape our world.

Architects in the twentieth century have manifested the Order of Dreams in several ways. Philip Johnson, an urbane gentleman and an architect of some means, has during the past twenty-five years made for himself a place of distinction in the landscape of Connecticut. (16) The various structures, assembled with consummate skill, each have a genealogy in the literature of architecture, just as Jefferson's did, and they are assembled with a fastidious care that is almost archeological.

The first and most famous building in the arcadian landscape of New Canaan was a totally glass-walled house. (17) Walls of glass were an especially potent literary as well as visual image in the development of Modern architecture, promising to prophets a new era of freedom and honesty. Johnson's

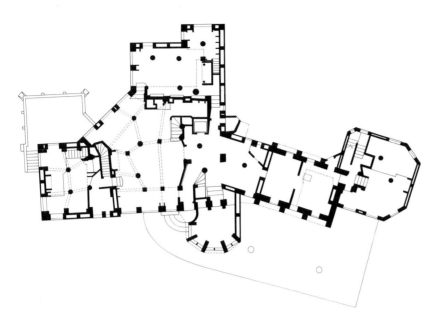

11. Plan, Fonthill (Mercer's castle), Doylestown, Pennsylvania, 1908–10

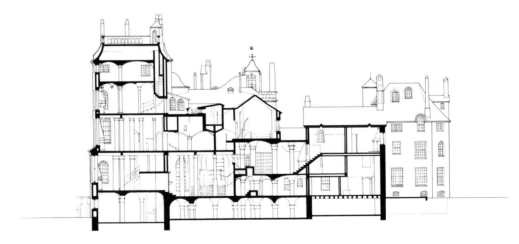

12. Section, Fonthill

13. Exterior, Fonthill

14. Morning room, Fonthill

15. Library, Fonthill

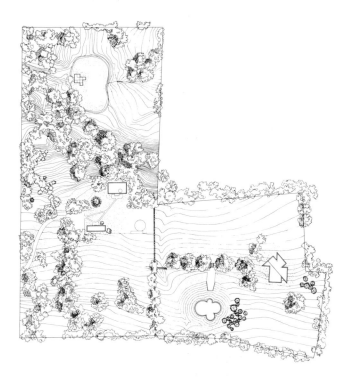

16. Site plan, Johnson house, New Canaan, Connecticut

17. Exterior, glass house, by Philip Johnson, 1949

disciplined structure is very like a crystal box. It captures the illusion of living in a fully transparent enclosure from which only the tawdry has been excluded. (18)

The guest house, an almost completely enclosed brick box, has its principal room enlivened by a free-standing vaulted arcade, recalling far-off seraglios, its exterior walls hung with shimmering gold curtains. (19) Outside and down the hill, still smaller vaults form a place for sheltered repose just above the surface of a pond from which a towering jet of water shoots. (20) Johnson's very considerable collection of paintings is enshrined in a crypt below ground, and his collection of sculpture in a separate glass-roofed pavilion. These buildings are disposed in the landscape in distinct, sculpted forms, a private Acropolis. Its buildings belong to, but are separate from, the land they claim.

In contrast, Frank Lloyd Wright, in the equally momentous house, Fallingwater, secured its owner's claim on the place by intimate involvement with the site, capturing and intensifying the natural ledging of rock and cave with the defiant thrust of human movement, with smooth concrete bridges crossing the crevice, darting up the hill, and balancing out over the falling stream. This house, like many others, includes reference to the traditional mythic elements of towers, caves, and formed land, but here the myth is held within a masterful composition. The house itself is a place to be explored as fully as the forested and craggy site which it has extended. Though dramatically different in appearance, it is at a deeper level like the place that it is in. (21–22)

These examples of works by architects are important not only because of the imagination and care they reflect, but also because the architects, in drawing from their personal experience, have been deeply

18. Interior, glass house

19. Bedroom, brick house, by Philip Johnson, 1949

20. *Pavilion, by Philip Johnson, 1962*

21. *Fallingwater, Bear Run, Pennsylvania, by Frank Lloyd Wright, 1936*

22. *Fallingwater*

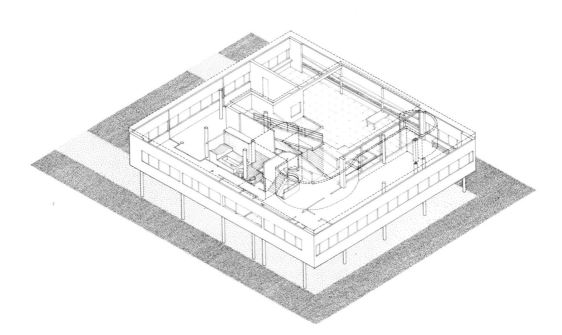

23. Villa Savoye, Poissy-sur-Seine, France, by Le Corbusier, 1929–30

concerned with the forms and images which have served as the language of expression in the architecture of the past.

Le Corbusier, no stranger to the study of architectural tradition, undertook as well to find meanings in the emerging forms of the society that surrounded him and to extract dreams from the technical achievements of his era. As editor of the magazine *L'Esprit Nouveau* he attempted also to formulate a way of living among the machines of modern times.

The Villa Savoye, often cited as an illustration of his dictum that a house is a machine to live in, has indeed a compelling relation to one of the most appealing machines of the twenties, the ocean liner. (23) The upper deck of the house is cast in forms reminiscent of the funnels and super-structures of ships. (24) There are analogies, too, in the taut shiplike skin of the outer walls, and the singular detachment of the whole house, which appears to be a pure white object floating in a pleasant green meadow. (25)

The house serves the dream of being onboard a ship. Living there must have been like being on a splendid sunbaked voyage. The main areas of the house are on the second level surrounded by thin and uniform walls which bind them together in a single volume to increase the sense of being removed from the land. Onboard, as it were, one is removed from the immediate site, unable to reach it or touch it except by descending through spaces that are strictly machine domains. Above, an open platform is the main focus, a deck for taking the air, for picnics and sunbathing. The fascination that Le Corbusier had for ships and the healthy life aboard them is transmuted in the Villa Savoye into support for the pleasures of a mechanically served life: machines in the service of hedonistic days.

24. Terrace, Villa Savoye

25. Exterior, Villa Savoye

139

The imagery was precise, yet disciplined by geometry and by care for the ways in which people live. The whole will carry meaning long after the specifics of its reference have been lost, because the dream of being in a place above the entanglements of daily life, with sun, air, and changing vistas to enjoy, is a specific framing of psychic longings that exist in each of us.

A complex of workers' houses in Pessac, near Bordeaux, designed by Le Corbusier to stringent budget requirements and for unknown inhabitants, carried much the same imagery, with cubic forms broken by stairs, decks, and loggias, and full-width windows stretched between bare stucco walls. (26) But the carefully constructed dreams that Le Corbusier had forged were either not recognized or not accepted by those who came to live there. These people looked instead for confirmation of their own image of a house. Over the years they have transformed Pessac's abstracted imagery into a much more familiar domestic vernacular. (27) The inhabitants, it seems, were especially concerned about the absence of two features characteristic of conventional houses in the region. Many felt they could not live in houses with front doors opening directly into the living rooms, which Le Corbusier had provided in order to make the most of the available space. Consequently a number of houses have had corridors carved out of the living rooms to accommodate the traditional pattern. (28) The most persistent difficulty in understanding the houses was, however, the absence of a visible roof. The provision of roof gardens and terraces on top of the flat roof was seen by some to be a benefit, but for many it simply did not match their expectations of what a house should look like. In a similar project at Lège, the roof terraces have all been covered over by traditional gable roofs. (29)

The extent of all this adaptation has seemed to many to indicate architectural failure. We think, on the contrary, that it represents the continuing efforts of residents to lay claim to their world in their own terms. Furthermore, it was indeed the generalized character of the initial design that allowed those who lived within these houses to enter into a continuing exchange with the buildings, to transform them to suit their own visions and wishes. Le Corbusier differentiated the machines of the house, planning the kitchen, bathrooms, and stairs with Pullman-like precision so that more space could be added to the main rooms of the house. It is those rooms and the open loggias and terraces—the empty stages for human action—that have become the location for personal differentiation and invention by the occupants.

More blameworthy are dwellings whose imagery is so totally controlled that there is no chance for the dwellers to make changes over the years, or even in the course of their daily lives. Such houses are unsuccessful. Similarly those which offer no suggestions to our dreams are unfulfilling. To have to consider each bolt as a bolt, not a rosette, the foot of each table leg as a point of distributed weight, not a lion's paw, each window as opening, not wall (or wall, not opening), each room as small, not big, is an impoverishment of life.

To extend your imaginative life into the everyday, the place that you live in should allow for the everyday to become exceptional. It should lead your mind to multiple associations. It should incorporate changing conditions of environment, of light, heat, air, and sound, so that your everyday rituals can be surprised by the exceptional conditions: sun-splattering reflections across the ceiling as it strikes a shiny teapot, a hot summer wind flapping

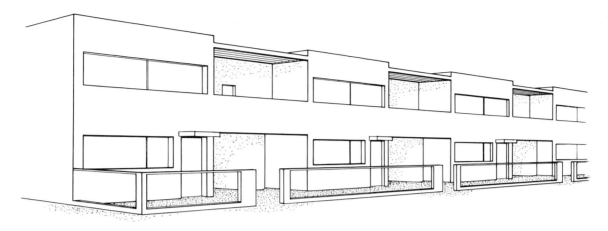

26. Housing at Pessac, by Le Corbusier (before)

27. Housing at Pessac (after)

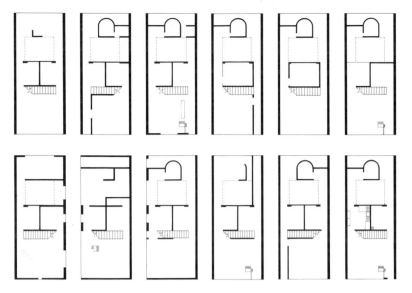

28. Plans, housing at Pessac (top, before; bottom, after)

29. A house at Lège, by Le Corbusier (top, before; bottom, after)

the window shades, the sound of water dripping in a spring thaw.

Not all the elements that touch our imaginations are exotic, nor need they all be grand. If you remain alert to your responses you will find the Order of Dreams present in the simplest of structures. The ways that a house lets you move, with grace or confusion, the shelters it puts around you, the things that it brings to your attention, all establish a substratum of meaning that accompanies the life you live there.

Many of the houses that we have shown are much larger and grander than those that we can afford. They, nevertheless, show that the Order of Dreams includes more than copying visual likenesses. The clues for fantasy and erudition, pretense and recollection are rooted deeply in the structure of a house. They must enter into the making of your house, as they do into the houses we have shown. Things as simple as stairs and level changes enter the Order of Dreams. They shape actions in obvious ways, and they imbue the house with the motions and gestures that have special meanings for you. These things specifically limit how you move, with what pace and how much effort; thus they show how you imagine yourself. Things to walk on, stand at, and sit on determine in great measure the dignity or casualness of your daily gestures, the easy slouch or the upright stance with which you approach the various encounters of the day. These influences are pervasive, yet we are seldom conscious of them. The actions that a house prompts form a part of our dreams.

Walls and their openings generally filter sensations, letting in the sun and breeze, or the sound of a waterfall, and sorting activities one from another, according to the social arrangements that prevail. They establish, by their degree of closure, their size, and by the particular aspects of the world they admit, those qualities that have to do with the dream of being sheltered and protected—the need to be inside *something* that motivates us all. Being inside a cave, inside a room, under a canopy, within a great domed enclosure, behind a fence, in an arena, on a balcony, or on a porch, all are conditions of enclosure which carry specific connotations. The forming of rooms and machine domains, and the relation of these to the landscape should be done with these variations of connotation in mind. They can be used to make special places within the house and to suggest their use.

Still the easiest and most prevalent means for expressing the Order of Dreams is display of the memorabilia of other times and places. In the architecture, not only of houses but of churches and public buildings, the most dramatic examples of display are often overhead. From the elaborate ceilings of Japanese palaces or the palace of Versailles to the painted vaults of Baroque churches and the pressed-tin ceilings of old American stores, builders have sought to develop their imagery above, where it would not interfere with the movement of people. These ceilings remind us that the life of the mind is not limited to the realm of immediate actions, and they indicate usefully a means by which our imaginations can be enriched without clogging the flow of practical events. They suggest that it is often wise to keep the myth up off the floor and, where possible, to build in such a way that the shapes which carry the visual imagery of a house can be largely independent of those which determine the actions of the place, except where those actions themselves can embody dreams. Much of what substitutes for these pleasures in houses built now is mere formalism, the empty repetition of shapes to which the inhabitants have no real connection, whose connotation they have not known and so cannot remember.

More likely to be relevant are the facts about the way buildings are built; the size of boards, the heaviness or complexity of spanning elements, the wiring, or the materials used where the house meets the dampness of the ground. These often claim the house for its builder or designer, but only vicariously for the occupant. To know how the builder used his materials, how he thought about them and acted with them is interesting, *if he cared*, as craftsmen of the past often did, and sometimes do now. However, the short cuts and indifference, the routine repetition of simple manufacturing, offer very limited nurture to the imagination, and you will need to bring personal elements of display to your house. The visible and communicative surroundings that a house establishes for your life should allow you to use your many capacities, to recognize, to remember, to discriminate, to analyze, to misinterpret, and to make fantasies.

Ask yourself what your mind is really set on. Is it the hot sun of the south playing on white walls and bright flowers or the dark, cathedraled forests of your memory? Is cozy clutter comfortable, or do you need cool, elegant, unbroken surfaces? Do you picture the gleam of brass or of parquet, or the acoustical-tile ceilings and green walls of the apartment you lived in when you were nine? Does the snap of screen doors, the whir of the lawn mower, or the buzz of an outboard motor bring a flood of memories?

What places have lurked in the recesses of your mind since first you saw them or read about them? Are they secret gardens or labyrinthine mazes, arches of triumph or alpine waterfalls, latticed porches or patios cooled by the splatter of fountains? Or, if you must, are they penthouses spacious enough for Fred Astaire and Ginger Rogers to grace with an impromptu foxtrot or staircases grand enough for Scarlett O'Hara to descend?

You must expose your dreams and fantasies. Luckily, perhaps, it is impossible to recreate them, or the environment for them, whole. The expression of dreams is accomplished by transmutation, developing the dream so that only its essence remains, and by miniaturization, reducing the pieces to a compass you can accommodate and afford. But what is left, transmuted, miniaturized, and fused with your other concerns, is the home for your imagination.

Setting out choices

Assembling the rooms

At this stage you should be able to identify your needs in terms of the Order of Rooms, which provide places for living, the Order of Machines, which assist you specifically in daily chores, and the Order of Dreams, which enrich the elements of the first two and give personal value to all the parts.

The next step will be to assemble all these parts to make the whole house. A good house is a single thing, as well as a collection of many, and to make it requires a conceptual leap from the individual components to a vision of the whole. The choices we will soon describe represent ways of assembling the parts. Each may be tried and tested, rejected or combined in the discovery of a way that will accommodate your needs comfortably and will also begin to create the place you want.

There is a general principle to guide you in the process, and it comes from the fact that a good house will have resonances that extend beyond a set of discrete elements. The principle is that, in the assembly of all the parts, *one plus one must equal more than two*. The execution of this principle to the fullest taxes skill and the imagination.

But in its simplest form it springs from a few very basic phenomena of building.

When, as we have noted, you make a room out of a floor, four walls, and a ceiling, you will have, besides those six things, a seventh as well: space, a thing probably more memorable than any of the physical elements that made it. Its creation, of course, is an illusion. You will not have made something out of nothing, only separated a particular part from the continuum of all space.

If, then, you arrange the rooms you have made in some kind of order, you will have not just a set of rooms, but you will also have given the whole house a pattern. If you let it, this pattern can tell much about you—your preference for formal living in a drawing room or for casual living in a family room or on a patio. It can suggest where you most often go when you first enter the front door, and where you like to cook. Pattern can also say more profound things about the kind of order which makes most sense to you—symmetrical, harmonious, and serene, or fragmented, jolting, and surprising.

Rooms, as they form the order of the inside, can, as another bonus, create outside domains. Houses whose rooms partially surround an interior courtyard, like many of the houses in Santa Barbara, show the most obvious way in which this can be done. But the more subtle arrangement of the three large houses on North Water Street in Edgartown, with rooms opening onto different parts of a shared lawn, perform similar acts of claiming the land around them. These claims are bought, as it were, for free, since they are achieved by means of the careful arrangement of parts (rooms) which were needed anyway.

What we have described are four simple exercises showing how the basic parts of a house can be put together to make more than just basic parts: they can also make *space, pattern, and outside domains.* They dramatize the most elementary act which architecture has to perform. To make one plus one equal more than two, you must in doing any one thing you think important (making rooms, putting them together, or fitting them to the land) do something else that you think important as well (make spaces to live in, establish a meaningful pattern inside, or claim other realms outside).

Two houses—one old and large, the other new and very small—can serve as illustrations of our principle. The first is Stratford Hall in Virginia, the home of the Lee family (page 86). Inside this house the rooms are assembled in an H-shaped plan that accommodated its occupants' daily activities in the two large wings and reserved enough room between them for the most formal room in the house, the Great Hall, which from its center gave vistas to the outdoors and spoke ceremoniously, as it still speaks, of a great family's sense of itself and its place both in society and on the land. The stairs which descend on each side from the Great Hall are the central elements of the two façades, which front the land—on one side a rolling greensward, some woods, and in the distance, the Potomac River (1), and on the other a flattened lawn and fields. (2) Heavy and dominant, the house claims the land and controls it. The way the rooms are assembled, the way the house is fitted to the land, and the manner and materials of which it is built, all render powerful bonuses and enhance the meaning of the house.

There is a bonus even in the eight chimneys, which are primarily there, of course, to vent the house's fireplaces. Once there, they also make a place for two commanding platforms between them, and as splendid shapes made of brick and mortar, they are the talismanic objects by which we are most likely to remember the house. (3) All the parts of Stratford Hall combine to create not only the house but also the dream of claiming, ordering, and controlling the land, and of making a special place to live. The rooms, the façades, the chimneys are all there to serve specific purposes, but together they enhance the whole.

Another example of the one plus one principle in operation is the Johnson house at the Sea Ranch. (4) An inexpensive West Coast vacation house, about one-fifteenth the size of Stratford, it has almost nothing in common with the Virginia mansion, save the economy of its concept, and the notion of making a symbolically important central space within.

The house sits high on a ridge of hills overlooking the shore, just where the forest gives way to open meadow and sweeping view of coastline. We and our clients wanted to make a tiny house with a sense at once of a mansion and of a country retreat. So, we built an imposing form in a simple and unimposing way.

1. *River front, Stratford Hall, Westmoreland County, Virginia, 1725*

2. *Plantation front, Stratford Hall*

3. *Stairs and chimneys, Stratford Hall*

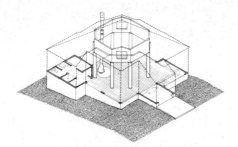

4. *Johnson house, Sea Ranch, California, by MLTW/Moore—Turnbull, 1966*

A drive through the forest ends at a redwood gate that opens onto a small flowered clearing, cultivated and tended, but not transformed into a separate garden alien from the Sea Ranch. On the far side of the clearing sits the house, fitted between a thicket of redwood and one of tanbark oak. From this side, under its pyramidal roof, it seems like a dollhouse, a simple geometric form with a central entrance porch. (5)

As you enter the double glass doors at the entrance and step up into the main room, you discover that the inside of the house is something the pyramidal roof outside didn't disclose: a surprising octagonal pavilion reminiscent of great halls, tombs, and bandstands in the park, but supported on plywood "cores," the cylindrical pieces left over when plywood has been peeled off in mills, locally available then for ninety cents each. (6)

Between the columns, the space of the central pavilion stretches into niches for specific purposes. Directly ahead is a nook for sitting and sleeping, with the fireplace to one side and a splendid view up the coast on the other. To the right as you enter, the room stretches into a domain for cooking, while on the left a place to eat is lodged between the posts of the octagon and the square corner. Behind the fireplace, on the far left, is a giant closet with a bathroom and dressing room.

Skylights just outside the four edges of the octagon emphasize its shape, surrounding it with constant soft light and surprising shafts of sunshine. This light from above illuminates the white walls, and therefore lessens the glare from the sea and sky, and frames the view of the outdoors. This one-room house seems at once a toy and the center of its own world, a retreat in the forest from which you can survey the coast.

At the Johnson house there was no space,

5. Exterior, Johnson house

6. Living area, Johnson house

no money, and really no need to make a separate room to which the other more utilitarian rooms were appended, as at Stratford. Though the house is just one room, it is a room of many dimensions. It provides places for a collection of specific activities and a judiciously wasted space, with its feeling of largeness.

The connection between the specific and symbolic areas is assured by the open spaces between the columns and, more subtly, by the four openings pierced in the octagon above. The distinction between the two realms of things is maintained with equal care, for the octagon in the middle is kept a separate thing, and it never touches the outside walls of the house even when it comes within a few inches of them, as it does behind the fireplace and in front of the large window. The alcoves around the edges, too, are not just dark closets appended to the central space, for they are flooded with light from the windows at eye level, and from the skylights above.

Each of the areas for specific use around the perimeter of the house, as well as the octagon in the center, with its feeling of half-mock grandeur, are in fact much too small to be either functional or effective alone. And so each borrows from the other in this miniature house, and each of the parts performs at least two separate tasks. Together, as at Stratford Hall, they make one plus one equal more than two.

Whateve: sleight of hand is involved in the process, houses are made, quite simply, from putting rooms together. Happily, for our purposes, the ways to assemble rooms are few. We count the following:

rooms linked
rooms bunched
rooms around a core
rooms enfronting the outside

plus two other patterns which occur when one room is given preeminence:

a great room within
a great room encompassing

Every memorable house we know of was formed in one of these six ways, or in a combination of them.

Rooms linked

Rooms can be lined up in a row, as in a little house in Portugal (7) Since this arrangement is so simple, it is memorable. Because covering the rooms in this scheme is the same thing as roofing the house, you can, if you choose, let the roof be the ceiling, and thereby reveal part of the structure of the whole house and also save money. The chances for lighting are ideal, too, since every room can have natural light from opposite sides. Its limitations are obvious: there is no circulation except through one room to another. If the house is small enough, this may present no problem, as in the Parson Capen house (page 72). Or if life is full enough of ceremony, even a large house like Lord Derby's in London could be designed as a series of rooms, most of which were lined up in single file. (8)

The most direct way of solving the circulation problems in a house where the rooms are linked is to insert a circulation space along one or both sides. A project by Robert Venturi is a good example of a set of rooms all in a row, alike and clear, "general in shape and unspecific in function," as he put it, separated by machine domains, with a porch on one side and an indoor passage along a part of the other (9), so that those rooms where the desire for privacy is anticipated can be bypassed, and those rooms where privacy is not an issue can simply be linked. To maintain the clarity of that linking the corridor is given

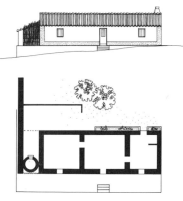

7. A small house in Portugal

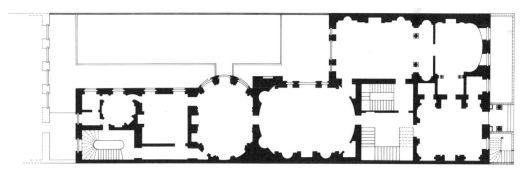

8. Lord Derby's house, London, by Robert Adam, 1777

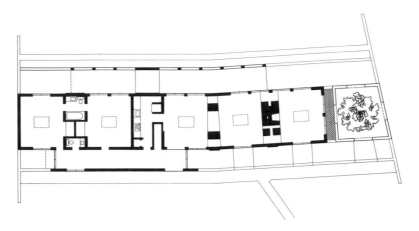

9. Pearson house (project), by Robert Venturi, 1957

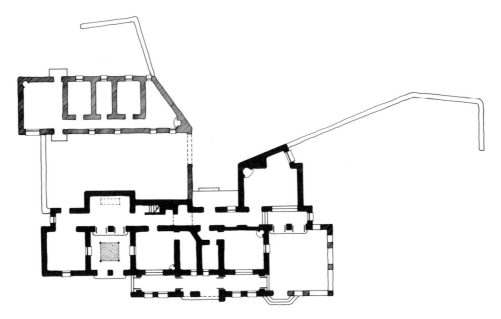

10. Jackson house (project), by MLTW/Lyndon, 1965

glass walls at each end, and the rooms are given great double ceilings which admit natural light at their top and all about their edges, to make as evident as possible the shape and importance of the rooms themselves.

A project of ours for a house in Sante Fe, New Mexico, depends similarly, though in the adobe idiom of the Southwest, on a single file of rooms along a passage. In this case, though, the passage extends the full length of the house. It is widened at one point to become an area for dining, and at one end it opens onto a sunken living room. (10) This house, like the Venturi project, emphasizes rooms linked, with an unroofed space, a garden, extending the chain at one end.

Another project for a house in England shows rooms linked together on two floors and connected by passageways that are sometimes corridors, sometimes a part of the rooms to which they allow access. (11) At the main entrance a windowed corridor leads to the kitchen, and in the other direction it opens up into the living area, two stories high. On the other side of the house a passageway leads from the living area and opens successively into the dining area, the kitchen, and at the end, a garden. Upstairs, a corridor above the first one connects the two bedrooms to the stairway behind the chimney.

The McElrath house, also two stories high (12–13), is composed of rooms linked both vertically and horizontally by a passage that climbs through a number of levels, dramatizing movement down past a dining area to a living room or, still in full view, up past a bridge to an intermediate level and finally to a skylit master bedroom at the top of the stairs. (14)

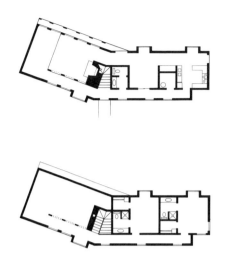

11. Vacation house (project), by Gerald Allen, 1972

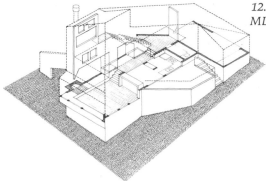

*12. McElrath house, Santa Cruz, California, by
MLTW/Moore–Turnbull, 1967*

13. Exterior, McElrath house

14. *Stairway, McElrath house*

Rooms bunched

A second method of arranging rooms is to bunch them; either they can be gathered around a central entry point or passage, or they can be bunched together completely with a passageway around them. Most houses of any size are organized according to this method, though generally it pushes the rooms together in ways which allow light to enter from only one side or two adjacent sides. Also, in this pattern, the act of covering a single room has nothing to do with roofing the whole house, so you must build a separate ceiling. An advantage of this way of assembling rooms is that it can accommodate them within a minimum perimeter.

The Portuguese house shown here is a simple example. (15) Its rooms are bunched together completely, and the larger rooms are sufficiently public to allow circulation through them to the smaller ones. One large room is unconnected with the rest of the house; it serves farm purposes.

The plan of a traditional Japanese house is admirably clear. (16) The sliding walls between rooms allow the relation of the one to the whole to become apparent. The whole house stays strongly in the mind, even as the three main rooms are themselves elegantly simple. They are carefully proportioned on the module of the three-by-six-foot tatami floor mat and have no permanent fixtures in them, so they are truly empty stages for human action. They are grouped beside an anteroom, arrived at through a small entrance garden. The anteroom itself, only about six feet square, gives directly through sliding panels onto two of the rooms. One of them adjoins the kitchen so is especially usable for dining. The other, a kind of reception room, has a garden view and a *tokonoma* in which to arrange a favorite picture and flowers or a bowl. At one

remove from the anteroom is a third room, which also opens through sliding screens onto the garden. At night the two rooms open onto the veranda along the garden front through which they have direct access to the toilet and so become favored sleeping rooms, as bedding is brought from the closets.

A larger Japanese house (17) is also composed of rooms bunched, this time around an interior passage which links all the rooms and is sufficiently strong and memorable itself to give a comprehensible position to each room it serves. The almost ritually planned movement of people entering and using the house is worth tracing. One comes in through a small entry, thence to an anteroom, which in turn opens onto the passageway. Just inside it, a stair up to a great room is on the left and the dining room to the right. Farther beyond to the right is a living room and to the left, a bathing suite and toilet. Straight ahead is a dressing room, normally open to the living room so that light comes from two sides. Still farther, and not at all a part of the system defined by the passageway, is the ceremonial tearoom and its kitchen.

The rooms, except for the tearoom, whose separateness is prized, are bunched, organized around a passage, but arranged, too, as with the living room and dressing room, so that the extent of the whole house can be seen, opening on opposite sides to its garden.

The room arrangements of these two Japanese houses are particularly easy to grasp because the rooms themselves are so empty and simple, and because the partitioning screens can slide open to reveal the shape of the whole house. An American house like Gunston Hall achieves its clarity of arrangement with much heavier and thicker materials, but the clarity is nonetheless striking (pages 72, 81). A central hall, entered from a

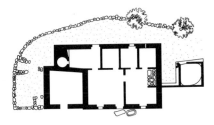

15. A small house in Portugal

16. A small house in Japan

17. A house in Japan

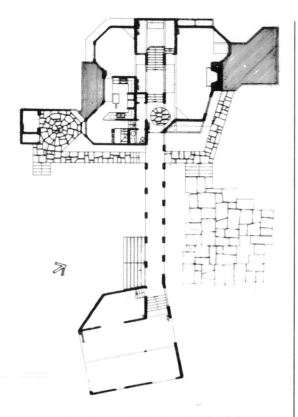

18. Tempchin house, Bethesda, Maryland, by
MLTW/Moore–Turnbull and Rurik Ekstrom,
1967

porch, extends all the way through the house past a staircase to a porch on the other side. On each side of the hall are two well-proportioned rooms, spacious in themselves, and gaining spaciousness from their connection with the central hall and from their vistas through it to the rooms on the other side. The rooms, roughly the same shape, are interchangeable. They can be simply visualized, and they build up in the mind's eye a memorable assembly of rooms bunched around the central hall.

The rooms in our Tempchin house are arranged around a central corridor in yet another way. (18) A long arcade, derived from what is locally called a "dog trot," leads from a carport at one end to the house at the other. On either side of the arcade the land falls away slightly. The roof slopes low over square openings toward the driveway, and high with tall openings to the lawn. (19)

Past the front door, these walls that flank the dog trot extend through the house. The passage opens above to a large square window seeking the sun (20) and sideways through syncopated openings to skylights or to the living room (21) and the dining room. (22) Directly ahead, it opens down into a sitting room above which an upper study is accessible from the living room.

This house is eclectic, carrying associations with many forms in the architecture of the past. The passage outdoors invites comparison with the arcades that reach to outbuildings in Palladian villas or in the farmhouses of Maryland and Virginia. The central brightly lit hall which extends the arcade with its multiple overlapping openings recalls, albeit in miniature and in the simplicity of sheetrock, the spatial complexities of plaster Bavarian churches.

Three other examples of rooms bunched follow: these pull the rooms completely together, and surround them with circulation. A word of caution should precede their examination: a circumferential passage consumes a large area, which is eligible, by most methods of reckoning, to be called waste space. Indeed, many state building agencies distinguish circulation spaces from rooms, and demand that a certain percentage of the total building area be the latter. This is thought to assure the efficient use of space. But the notion of efficiency of this sort is suspect in a house, since a great deal of the space in houses, in rooms as well as passages, is for circulation—the opportunity for human movement. Comparatively little space is required, for instance, for a seated group engaged in conversation or for people sleeping in bed. Understandably, there is wastefulness in corridors if they are useless except for walking through and unpleasant even for that. But the passage in a house like Homeplace Plantation (page 75) is more than a corridor. During warm weather, it is probably the most useful room in the house, serving as a place to sit, or read, or nap, or play, or keep accounts, and to catch whatever breeze is blowing. The inner rooms lose some privacy, but gain in shade.

The Japanese house (23) has a circumferential passage not altogether unlike Homeplace Plantation's, except that another layer of rooms outside it—nursery, dressing room, maid's room, kitchen, bath, toilet, and old people's room—cause the passageway to be sometimes an interior one, sometimes a veranda. Because of the openness of the sliding screens, the passageways, which are too narrow to provide sitting space, take the pressures of movement off the central rooms so the latter can be used just for sitting, sleeping, and staying and, at the same time, have vistas across the veranda to the garden.

On a much grander scale, the Ninomaru at Nijo Castle (24) in Japan is spectacularly

19. *Exterior, Tempchin house*

20. *Central passage, Tempchin house*

161

21. *Living room, Tempchin house*

22. *Dining room and central passage, Tempchin house*

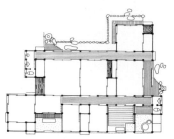

23. A house in Japan

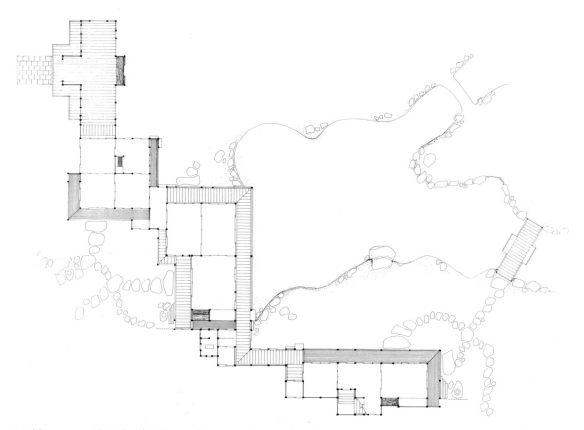

24. Ninomaru, Nijo Castle, Kyoto, Japan, early seventeenth century

formed of four sets of rooms bunched with
perimeter circulation, all in an irregular row.
This arrangement provides a number of
corner rooms inside the veranda, placed to
receive broad views and whatever breezes
cool the soggy Japanese summers. The
wood-floored veranda became a space of
great importance as a gathering place for the
many attendants of the court, and as a path
to conduct the visitor from the closed porch
at the lower right, where he entered, to
whatever audience hall or living room his
station entitled him.

Rooms around a core

A third method of arranging rooms is to
wrap them around a core. The core can be
a solid one, like the chimney in the Parson
Capen house (page 72) or the Ward Willitts
house (pages 77–78). The core can also be a
collection of machines and their domains, as
in the Gross cabin. (25) The central stair
looks over the kitchen equipment into a
high, brightly lit room used for cooking,
eating, and lounging. This is adjoined,
outside, by a large porch whose edge
runs parallel to the core, but diagonal
to the room, ending in steps that lead down
into the meadow. In this house in the North
Woods, machines that make heat—the stove
and the fireplace—are bunched back to back
at the corner of the stair and adjoining the
rest of the core. Under the master bedroom
and in front of the fireplace is a low,
protected room with carpeted platforms and
recesses that face the fire and the two bay
windows. On the other side of the machine
core two children's bedrooms open into each
other and join with the space at the foot of
the stairs to make a small play area.

The rooms can also be wrapped around
an open space. The larger houses in Ur of
the Chaldees of the period just after 2000
B.C. are arranged in this way (26), and it was

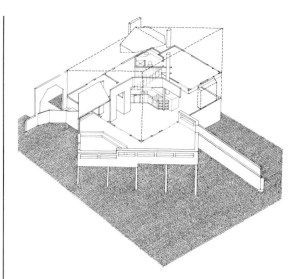

25. *Gross house, Hartland, Vermont, by
MLTW/Lyndon, 1971*

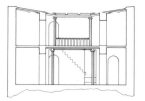

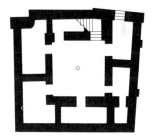

26. *A house in Ur of the Chaldees, ca. 2000 B.C.*

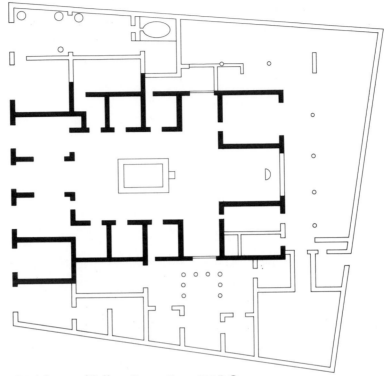

27. A house of Sallust, Pompeii, ca. 100 B.C.

standard for many Greek and Roman houses. (27)

The arranging of rooms around an open space has some special advantages; as with rooms linked in a row this scheme can give each room light and air from both sides. In addition, it can give privacy from the outside world, though not much interior privacy is provided if the rooms open into the same court. By being one-room deep, it provides another advantage in that supporting the roof of the room and the roof of the house are the same act, and perceiving the relation of the parts to the whole is made easier. Another enormous advantage, which will be more fully noted in the section on fitting the house to the land, is the ease with which the house can back against other houses, or against property not belonging to the house.

The disadvantages of the scheme are the inaccessibility of the courtyard to breezes and the sheer number of rooms required to surround an open space of any size, though it is certainly possible for rooms to join with freestanding walls or adjacent buildings to surround an outdoor space.

A house in Cuernavaca, Mexico, has rooms which partially surround an open space, though the enclosure is completed by the blank exterior wall of the house next door. (28) The surrounded space is a garden; along it on two sides an open gallery provides, in the benign Cuernavacan climate, the main room in the house, both for moving and for sitting. (29) The master bedroom intercepts the gallery, but has two doors which, when they are open, continue the space visually past the bedroom, beyond a swimming pool, to a loggia at the back of the site, which serves as a porch for a guesthouse bordering a third side of the garden. The other rooms, a living and dining room, a kitchen and service area, and a guest room, all open onto the gallery. They are used chiefly when privacy is desired or when inclement weather makes the gallery too cold or windy.

The Goldenberg house (30) by Louis I. Kahn is another courtyard house, but it contains rooms and circulation spaces of various sizes and shapes constructed in a variety of ways. Unlike the Mexican example, this is a free standing house, so major rooms face both out and in. But the clarity of the central open square gives it preeminent importance in the house. Our project for the Jenkins house, with rooms which can be opened wide to the court during the long dry summers in the Napa Valley, is another variation on the same scheme. (31)

The Shokin-tei teahouse at Katsure Villa in Japan is also a freestanding structure, distinguished by its wide eaves and verandas which unite it with the splendidly developed landscape around. In its middle—surprisingly—is an inner court, unroofed and visible only from the ceremonial tearoom, so that instead of being central it seems extremely remote. (32)

In a house in Portugal the surrounded space is more like a private street, which cuts through the house from front to back, making at once a patio and an outdoor corridor. (33) At its center it opens into a covered space which contains a well, and makes a proper patio. The form is considerably more open to the public street than the standard courtyard plan, which usually requires one to go through the house itself in order to reach the central open space.

The possibilities of varying the shape of this space, and the precise configuration of the rooms wrapped around it, are of course legion, but the basic arrangement of rooms wrapped around a central core has been probably the most important organizational scheme in the history of house building.

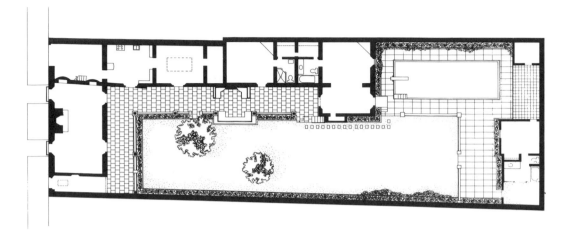

28. A house in Cuernavaca, Mexico

29. Gallery of a house in Cuernavaca

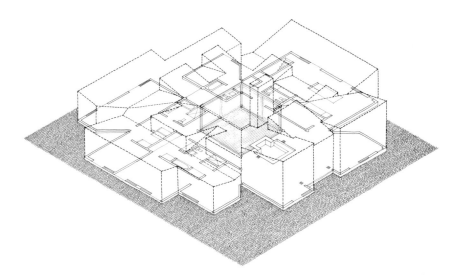

30. *Goldenberg house (project), by Louis I. Kahn, 1958*

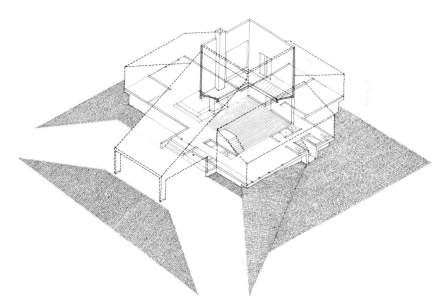

31. *Jenkins house (project), by MLTW, 1963*

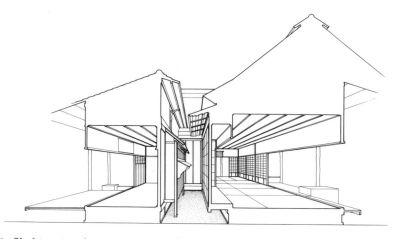

32. Shokin-tei teahouse, Katsura Villa, Kyoto, Japan, early seventeenth century

33. A house in Portugal

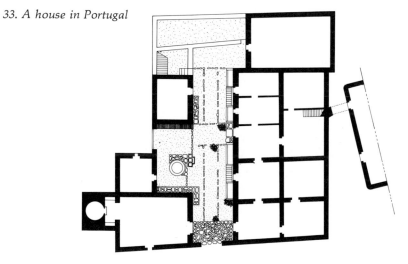

Rooms enfronting the outside

A fourth scheme for organizing rooms is one in which rooms are marshaled along a line to *face* some part of the out-of-doors beyond themselves. We call this arrangement of rooms *enfronting*.

In one example, rooms of two levels of importance are arranged to enfront a public space. The main room, in the center, and two rooms of slightly less importance face the front of the building, while subsidiary rooms behind open to the major rooms. This design sprang from the decision to face one particular piece of the outside—in this case, a public square—and to turn the important rooms to it, much as one would line up a military guard for inspection, with the most important or brilliantly plumaged members out in front. (34)

Charles Bulfinch's third Harrison Gray Otis house in Boston is memorable for the simple and dignified way its rooms enfront the street. (35) But as the plan discloses, the room arrangement becomes more and more loose and informal toward the back of the lot. Indeed here, as in many elegant Georgian town houses in England, the casual arrangement of the back of the house is altogether different from the grand scale of the rooms which face the street. In this way, the rooms can be a part of a number of different realms, from that larger realm of the out-of-doors—whether a lawn sloping to the river, or a city street, or a park—to a much more intimate realm of domestic courtyards.

A plan of several houses in the Circus at Bath shows another variation on this way of assembling rooms. The curving front is formal and highly disciplined, while on the back the rooms, when necessary, bulge outward without any particular regard for what they will look like from outside. (36) On the front or back, all the rooms are clear

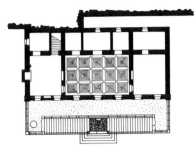

34. A house in Portugal

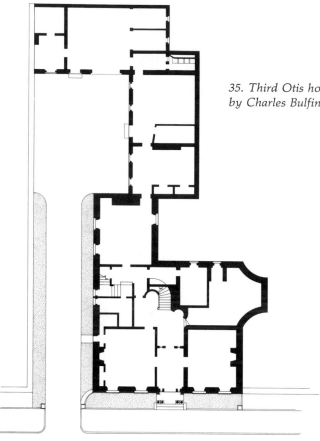

35. *Third Otis house, Boston, Massachusetts, by Charles Bulfinch, 1806*

36. *Houses in the Circus, Bath, England, by John Wood the Elder, 1754*

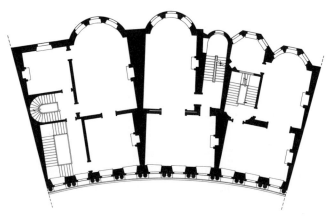

and symmetrical in shape, even though that required extensive accommodations to the irregularity of the curving structure. The space of the rooms and the shape of the whole was obviously of far more interest to the eighteenth-century builders than the way the whole house was put together.

The distinguishing characteristic of rooms enfronting the outside is that they are arranged in relation to something beyond themselves, and the chief advantage of this arrangement is that it allows the rooms to have an outlook over whatever they face and share its qualities. By the same token, it is only useful if there is something worth facing: either something already there; or something made and shared, like the greenswards in front of the row houses in Bath; or something private, like one's own garden.

A great room within

So far we have talked of rooms of roughly equal importance, linked or bunched or wrapped around a core or enfronting the outside. The two other ways a house can be put together involve the invention of something more than an individual room, of greater import than any of the rest of the rooms. Such rooms have had varying names in the past, and each name leaves a residue of specific images: great hall, *salle*, *sala*, long gallery. We shall describe them as Great Rooms within the house and as Great Rooms capable of encompassing the whole house.

Stratford has a Great Room within, though it does not open directly into any other room, and the other rooms retain their independence. (37) Even so, one's memory of the house centers on that Great Room. Palladio's villa plans (38) are frequently organized around a Great Room onto which the other rooms do open. This room

provides the basis for arranging everything else—rooms surrounding a Great Room, rooms flanking a Great Room, or bunches of rooms flanking a Great Room.

At Chiswick House, as in the Palladian villas on which it is modeled, a Great Room stands in the center. (39) Chiswick was built by Lord Burlington, one of eighteenth-century England's most erudite patrons of the arts. Guests would enter the central hall and then be ushered according to their interests to the left, or right, or on behind into one of the rooms where poetry, or art, or humanist sentiments were under discussion. The plan of the house shows how importantly the Great Room figured as a circulation space through the pavilion to its other rooms, symbolically, as well as by being the largest, highest, and most important single space in the whole house.

A great room encompassing

Houses from the past seldom exhibit our sixth system for assembling rooms, a Great Room encompassing, within which particular functions and even other rooms are accommodated. Philip Johnson's glass house in New Canaan, Connecticut, is a particularly clear example of such a scheme; it is basically a single room, readily retained in the memory because of its simple shape and its all-glass walls. (40) We see it, and we remember it as an open glass box; but inside there is a brick cylinder, enclosing a bath and a fireplace, and two blocks, enclosing kitchen machines. These modify and control the space, and create areas for specific use and privacy inside the crystalline Great Room.

Japanese houses, because of the flexibility of their partitions and the strong form of their roofs and verandas, often qualify as single encompassing Great Rooms. Each of the pavilions at Nijo is a Great Room, with

173

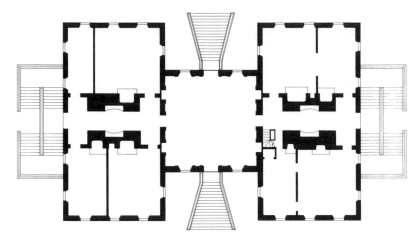

37. Stratford Hall, Westmoreland County, Virginia, 1725

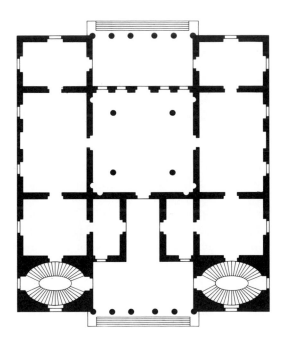

38. Villa LVII (project), by Andrea Palladio, 1570

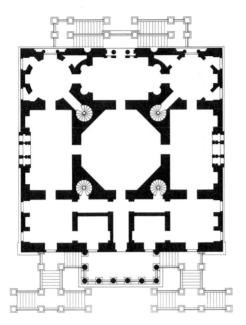

39. Chiswick House, by Lord Burlington, Chiswick, England, 1729

40. Glass house, New Canaan, Connecticut, by Philip Johnson, 1949

a clear perimeter and an arrangement inside sufficiently light and flexible not to stand in the way of remembering and responding to the whole (page 164).

Our own houses, especially the small ones, have relied heavily on the use of an encompassing Great Room. The condominiums at the Sea Ranch, for example, are single volumes with large structures inside to hold all the machines, including the sleeping lofts (page 37).

There are, then, six ways of putting rooms together on one or several stories. We know of no more, save their combination. The most difficult part of the design of a twentieth-century house, though, occurs in the area where the generalized rooms meet the special domain of the machine.

Including the machines

Our houses are filled with machines and the domains required for their comfortable use. Accommodating them and at the same time maintaining a coherent assembly of rooms is particularly taxing. Nevertheless, we know of just four ways in which the Order of Rooms and the Order of Machines can be juxtaposed without confusion, and they are:

Forming the rooms around machines
Putting the machines inside the rooms
Putting the machines outside the rooms
Sandwiching the machines between the rooms

Forming the rooms around machines
Frank Lloyd Wright's Goetsch-Winkler house is formed almost entirely around machines. It was built in 1939 in Okemos, Michigan, and was one of a group of houses with which he hoped to develop a pattern for the small suburban house. (1)

Here the machines and their domains create the house, rather than being separate elements in it. The dining table, which flows out from the wall, the work table, the built-in seat by the fireplace, as well as the bar, the toilet, the sink and the refrigerator and the storage shelves—all are machines designed for a specific purpose and anchored in place. (2)

They are not only fixed in the space: they fix the space. All of the machines and the domains around them create areas of specific use which delimit the flowing space of the living rooms and the corridor. Even the major space is formed by them.

In the Goetsch-Winkler house the living spaces are *machine specific*. The house is made up of elements which are each tightly fitted to a particular activity, machined as it were, to a very specific and limited number of actions.

Putting the machines inside the rooms
A condominium unit at the Sea Ranch illustrates an opposite approach. (3) Though admittedly a vacation house and therefore simpler than a year-round residence, it shows in one way what results from rigorously separating machines and their domains from rooms. Here the machines are placed in a compact tower set in the midst of a more casually composed living space. In the crawl space beneath the floor is the furnace.

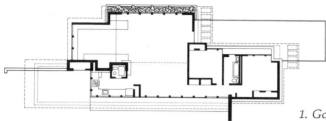

1. Goetsch-Winkler house, Okemos, Michigan, by Frank Lloyd Wright, 1939

2. Interior, Goetsch-Winkler house

3. Condominium unit 9, Sea Ranch, California, by MLTW, 1966

On the main floor are a stove, refrigerator, sink, dishwasher, and kitchen storage; on a balcony above is a sink and a closet adjacent to a private space that contains a toilet and a bathtub. At the top is a bunk bed, a more primitive kind of machine, and the whole tower is laced about with still other simple machines—a ladder and some stairs, underneath the lowest of which is the water heater.

Even the telephone, the thermostat for the furnace, and the switches and dimmers for most of the lights in the house are located in this central machine core, so that there is an evident order and a simplicity to the whole, although its actual appearance is rather complex. The clarity and, above all, the specificity of this arrangement was of great concern to us, for as we have already noted, it allows the remaining area of the condominium to be a room pure and simple, a large stage.

Another house of ours, the Karas house in Monterey, California, has a machine of another shape right at its center. (4) The Karases, with all but one of their children grown, liked the wooded part of Monterey they lived in, but were tired of their large conventional ranch house. They asked us for a design which would allow them freedoms of spirit which their old house dampened. They owned a pleasant wooded lot at the edge of a forest, with a view over Monterey Bay; and they were anxious to keep to a budget which might maintain their high spirits in financial realms as well. (5)

The house is compact and almost square in plan. On the ground floor, a square doughnut of rooms surrounds a one-story block (the "machine") which contains fireplace (6), powder room, a small kitchen, a stair, and a furnace. On top of this block is a platform suitable for musicians, who are very much in evidence in this household.

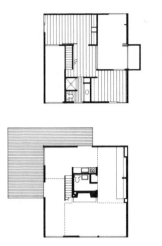

4. *Karas house, Monterey, California, by MLTW/Moore–Turnbull, 1967*

5. *Exterior, Karas house*

6. Fireplace, Karas house

At the second-floor level, alternate corners
are enclosed for two bedrooms and a bath,
all entered off the musicians' platform.
And higher still, at the top of a ladder, is
a sleeping platform for adventurous guests.

The house is extraordinarily high, and in
the two corners where there is no second-
floor room the space goes up to the exposed
rafters. On the north wall (7) a window
above high bookshelves looks out onto a
box painted white, which reflects sunlight
into the house. A bright yellow painted
circle acts as a surrogate sun, doubly
unexpected on the north side and in this
cool and often foggy forest.

Putting the machines outside the rooms
Another approach to the wedding of rooms
and machines can be seen in the Bonham
cabin in the Santa Cruz Mountains, which
we have already described. In it the kitchen
and bathroom are so small, so specific, that
they become in our terms machine domains,
and are in saddlebag lean-tos attached to
the one main room of the house.

The same approach, in a totally different
time and place, was used in a design of a
vacation house for an English conductor and
scholar who wanted a house for work as
well as leisure away from London. (8) The
site chosen is a two-acre rectangle bounded
on one side by a village lane, on another
by a hedgerow blocking the view to the
neighboring farmer's pig pen, and on another
by a splendidly expansive view east across
the Hollandesque landscape of Norfolk.
On the south and final side, the neighbor
is a handsome but simple thirteenth-century
parish church, whose original stained-glass
windows have been replaced by clear ones
so that from the site there is a view not only
of the church but through it as well.

The little house consists of two tall brick
masses at right angles to each other, white-

7. *Sun window, Karas house*

8. *Leppard house (project), by Gerald Allen, 1970*

washed, and with their sloping roofs covered with red concrete tiles—a common and cheap building material in Britain. Into the angle and facing the view and the church, a Great Room is nestled. It looks rather like a quartered gazebo, and is made of wood and glass with a tin roof.

In this house, as in the Bonham one, the other rooms—here a study, kitchen, stair hall, two tiny bedrooms and baths—are sufficiently small to be regarded as machine domains, and they flank the Great Room on two sides of the house.

Both houses are reduced, eroded versions of the idea of the Great Room within. In their cases, though, unlike the cases of the Italian and English Palladian palaces we have described, the Great Room is simply the only room, the only empty stage for human improvisation. What is left over, the specifics, are consigned to adjacent machine domains.

The advantage of this arrangement is its simplicity and economy. Instead of a series of moderately sized rooms, too small for much improvisation and too large for most specific activities, both houses provide one generous room and, clearly and separately defined, a group of machine domains.

Sandwiching the machines between the rooms

Two other houses which we have discussed already provide examples of the final way we know to join rooms and machines.

Robert Venturi's project for a house in Chestnut Hill lines all the rooms and machines up in a row, first a room, then a machine, then a room, and so on. Louis Kahn's Goldenberg house project, following a more complex set of requirements, layers the rooms and machines around the central courtyard in a less immediately perceived, but equally distinct order (page 169).

Our house for the William Jewell family in Orinda, California, is another example of a room and machine sandwich. (9-10) Mrs. Jewell is from New England and was not much enamored of California indoor-outdoor living. Though she wanted the clarity and separateness of good Georgian rooms, and had a scrapbook full of fine New England houses, she did not want to shut out or deny the particularly gentle and sunny climate in the valley behind the hills east of San Francisco Bay. Nor did she want the hot, uncomfortable, and faintly prickly sensation which the uncompromised reproduction of "Georgian" houses creates in these climes.

Our response was to make four rooms, smooth-walled and simply shaped, opening onto a set of porches and bays more roughly finished and from there to the outside. (11) Bathrooms and laundry are sandwiched between the rooms on the first and second floors, leaving the main rooms clearly defined, although one, a large cooking room, has machines within it.

The virtue of sandwiching is that it allows for a set of rooms of similar size, assembled in rather traditional ways, unbroken and unspoiled by the unwanted intrusion of machines and their domains.

Accommodating the automobile

Once the assembly of rooms and machines has been considered, it is worth noting the problem of connecting the whole house to that special machine, the automobile. Is it a friend?—in which case you admit it; or a foe?—in which case you exclude it. Do you need to step from your car into your house under cover immediately, or do you prefer to leave the world of the road behind and walk some distance to the house? Should the automobile arrive at the front door or back, or both places? What form of shelter,

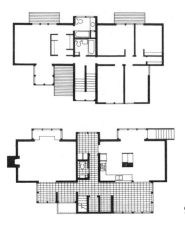

9. Plan, Jewell house, Orinda, California, by MLTW, 1964

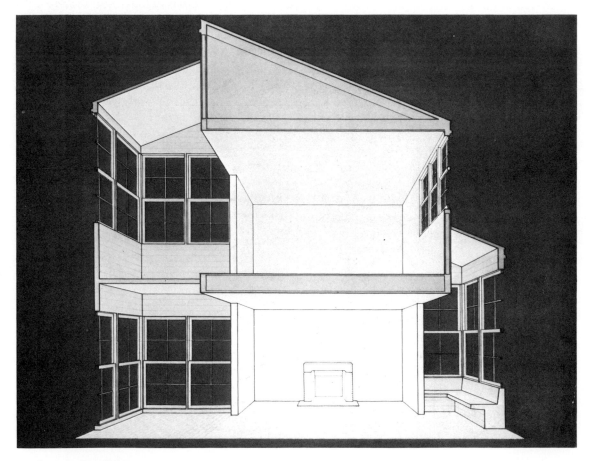

10. Section, Jewell house

11. Exterior, Jewell house

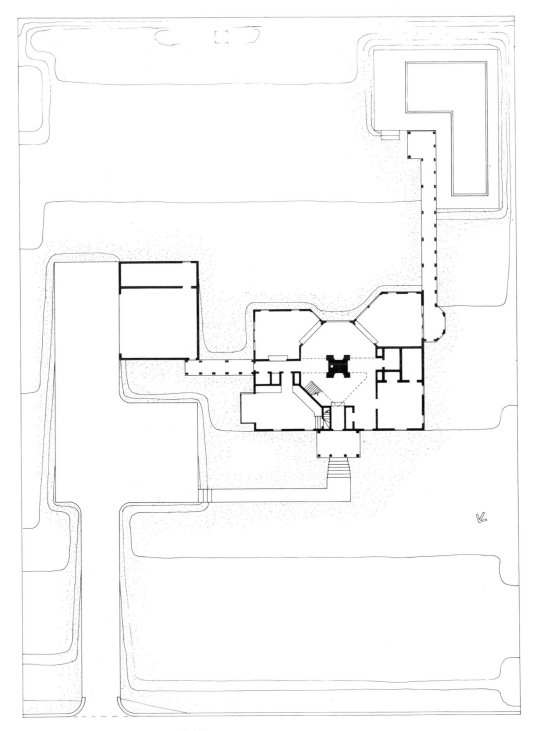

12. *Smyth house (project), by Gerald Allen, 1972*

if any, does it need: a garage, a carport, or just plastic wrapping?

In answering these questions it is important to note as well that the farther from the public road the car travels the more it will cost to prepare a route for it, and that the more you build to shelter it, the less you will be able to build to shelter yourself. Consider what else you can do with the shelter, what other machines might share this domain, or how the space, when it is empty, might, for example, sometimes be a place for children's games or theatricals. Remember, too, how the structures which shelter the car may also help configure the site, and also affect the relationship between the public world of the road and the private world of the house. For houses which are isolated and remote the automobile is, in effect, a kind of mobile porch.

As we have already noted, at the Johnson house at the Sea Ranch the automobile is excluded by a large redwood fence between the parking area and the house. The fence has a sliding door in it, which opens, with only a little effort, enough for people to pass through. With a bigger push, it opens more to let cars or trucks enter when necessary. This fence is not only a screen between the cars and the house, it also screens the house from the road. The screen makes a sheltered enclosure that contrasts to the spectacular views of the Pacific from the other side of the house.

Another solution is used in many of the houses in Santa Barbara, which have a walled entry court into which the automobile can pass and stop either at the front door or in a carport.

In more densely populated suburbs, though, there is usually a blatant inconsistency in the way the automobile is allowed to approach the house. Once, as we have seen in Edgartown, houses in American towns nestled up close to the street, and with a prominently placed doorway they invited entrance. "Traditional" houses in our suburbs, now set far back from the street, still follow this pattern, as though the car had never been invented. Since it has, the result is that the carefully formed front door for pedestrian entrance almost never gets used, and nearly everyone comes into the house from a garage or carport, and after tripping over rakes, lawn mowers, and roller skates, winds up in the kitchen.

A short-term remedy to this problem can be seen in the site plan of the Smyth house, in North Carolina. Here, in somewhat grudging concert with its stolid suburban neighbors, the house enfronts the street from the vantage of its required seventy-five-foot setback. It is realistically presumed, though, that everyone will arrive at the house by car, and so an ample driveway is built up to the house. Near its end a set of parking spaces is provided for visitors, and a set of steps and a walkway invite them to the front door. For the owners the driveway continues into the garage, which is connected to the house by an arcade leading, not into the kitchen, though near it, but into the central hall of the house. (12)

Another remedy is to place the front door near the garage so that the part of the house which invites entrance most strongly can also accommodate the most likely mode of arrival.

We have, then, in our search for clarity, some fairly simple categories: six kinds of room arrangement, four ways of introducing machine domains, twenty-four basic combinations.

Next comes the chance, with four ways of fitting the house to the land, to bring to over eighty the plausible, but still unembroidered, schematic possibilities.

187

Fitting the house to the land

Assembling the rooms and machines into a coherent pattern for a house provides only the beginnings. As you examine the basic combinations we have set forth, you must also consider the special opportunities and problems posed by the site you have, and understand the ways a house can fit the land. Then the real shape of the house can emerge, taking its special place in the landscape or on a street.

Houses exist in a bewildering variety of sites and environmental conditions, of course, and these affect the house you build. Nevertheless, we can still identify just four ways to fit a house to the land: by merging, claiming, enfronting, and surrounding.

Merging

When hills or trees or other textures are strong on a site, the house can be made to blend into the landscape and seem a part of it. Though it is man-made, it can give the impression of being at one with its surroundings, and consonant with them. (1) The houses on the wooded hills at the Sea Ranch, for instance, merge with their sites.

Claiming

Claiming is the opposite of merging; it occurs when the house is a clear and strong shape, set in contrast to the land around it. (2) The house seems what it is, man-made and intentionally different from its natural setting. From this juxtaposition a curious phenomenon occurs: the house seems to have the power to claim as its own a part of the land around it. A strong shape prominently placed, like a fortress on a mountaintop, can dominate, in fact as well as in the mind's eye, enormous horizons. Domestic buildings, like the gray shingled houses on the beach in Edgartown, also have this power to claim impressive vistas. Less dominant houses on smaller plots, like the old houses on North Water Street in Edgartown, stake a strong claim only on the land close around them.

Enfronting

A building with an imposing facade enfronts a part of the land, usually a street, or a square, or a plaza, or even a particular view. (3) Enfronting the site requires one face of a house to be made special in order to address a certain feature of the site. It is distinct from the way the rooms inside are assembled, since they can be put together to enfront one thing while the building itself enfronts something else in a different direction. The rooms in many houses in Charleston, for example, enfront the long garden beside the house while the entrance side of the house itself enfronts the street.

Surrounding
This mode of siting is the direct parallel of rooms surrounding an open core. Elements of the house close around a part of the land to make a private domain outdoors. (4) The closure may be only partial, or it may be complete, accomplished either by the house itself or the house and an adjacent garden or courtyard wall, as in Santa Barbara. If it is complete, the result is an interior courtyard which can be transformed, as the lush patios of many desert houses are, into a private open space different from the rest of the outdoors.

Surrounding is an intensified version of claiming, where the act of claiming is turned inwards.

The choice among these possible ways of fitting the house to the land will be made in part because of the limitations of the particular site in question—its size and location, its view, slope, exposure to sun and wind and neighbors, the texture of natural growth, and the climate. Not all four of the possibilities are equally well suited to all sites.

Rural sites as a class offer more possibilities than sites in cities or suburbs, since rural sites exist which can accommodate any of the siting modes—merging, claiming, enfronting, and surrounding—and sometimes more than one at once.

If a site in the country is filled with trees, rocks, hillocks, and undergrowth,

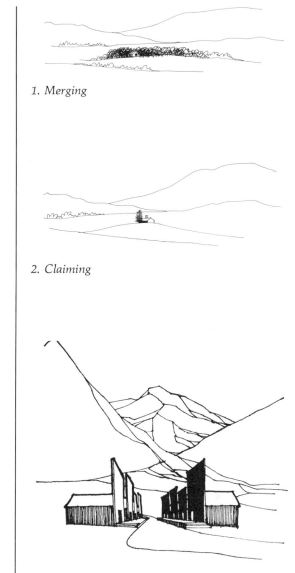

1. Merging

2. Claiming

3. Enfronting

4. Surrounding

merging will be an obvious possibility, and in fact will happen almost by itself. If these natural textures are very strong, it may be impossible to avoid merging, unless you are willing to clear away some of the trees and undergrowth, and alter the terrain.

A house on open rural land can also be made to merge with its background by keeping its profile horizontal or low. One of the most celebrated examples of this technique is Frank Lloyd Wright's Taliesin West. (5) A more modest example is our Shinefield house at the Sea Ranch. (6) We dug it and its terrace into the ground, and bulldozed berms of earth around it, then gave it a roof partly of sod to reinforce the merger.

It is also possible to make houses on open land merge with their background by placing them near or against some prominent feature of the terrain. We noted in our chapter on the Sea Ranch that Joseph Esherick did this with his series of houses nestled close by the cypress break, with their shed roofs placed so as to offer least resistance to the strong winds blowing in off the Pacific.

The opposite of merging, claiming, can be used on large rural sites, since claiming occurs most spectacularly where there is a good deal of land to be claimed.

Claiming is possible when a house is unobscured by trees or hills or other buildings, and when its shape or color stand out against landscape. The strength with which a house makes its claim on the land depends on the size and shape of the house itself, and as well on the vastness of the landscape and the number of other competing buildings.

A single small house in the vacant landscape can have extraordinary prominence and power (7). On a landscape that is more varied and more broken up into a number

5. *Taliesin West, near Phoenix, Arizona, by Frank Lloyd Wright, 1938*

6. *Shinefield house, Sea Ranch, California, by Charles Moore Associates and Dimitri Vedensky, 1971*

7. *A farmhouse near Manhattan, Kansas*

of separate parts, a shape of greater size and prominence is required to dominate it. Stratford Hall is an example. Its claim on the land is assured in part by its clean and strong shape and strengthened by the long swath cut through the surrounding trees down to the river.

Forts, and even more obviously Greek temples, show that if a building in an open rural landscape is also on top of a hill, its power to claim the land all around and below it is increased. This power must come not only from its heightened visibility but also because hilltop sites are associated in our minds with places of sacred or strategic importance. In any case, it is a pervasive power, possessed as well by totally domestic buildings like Monticello, which from the top of its little mountain manages to command considerable horizons even though parts of that landscape today are cluttered with other buildings.

A house on an open rural site can also enfront some particularly important feature of the land. Palladio's sixteenth-century villas, generally built for gentlemen farmers on the Venetian mainland, often enfronted the land which was the source of their owner's wealth. Loggias and arcades extended the line of contact with the land. (8) America's most familiar example of enfronting is Mount Vernon, where a two-story porch with thin columns enfronts the Potomac River from a high bluff. (9)

Surrounding, the fourth mode of fitting a house to the land, is less frequently used on rural sites than the other three, possibly because it generally implies turning away from the landscape and making a smaller, more special outdoors in the center of the house. Sometimes, as in the desert, this turning away is desirable and even necessary. Sometimes, as in Mexican haciendas, it is part of a cultural tradition.

8. *Villa XXXI (project), by Andrea Palladio, 1570*

9. *River front, Mount Vernon, Fairfax County, Virginia, 1785*

10. The Shambles, York, England

Dense urban sites, surprisingly, offer almost as many possibilities for fitting a house to the land as rural sites do, though the act of fitting here involves relating to a man-made urban fabric, rather than to a natural texture of terrain and trees.

Merging can be achieved in cities by making a building casually like its neighbors, and this has been done with greater or less skill for centuries. (10) Claiming necessarily requires more land whether it be green lawns or broad expanses of pavement, and so in cities it is a mode which is often reserved for public buildings of unusual importance or, lately, for corporate headquarters.

In many Western countries tradition has required houses on small plots of land to enfront the street. The false-front buildings in Western American towns at once spring to mind as a straightforward example. (11) But any number of houses in towns in Britain and some in America provide more elegant versions. (12) In some cases, as we have already seen, the building may enfront the street, just as Georgian row houses do, but the rooms inside enfront some other part of the site. (13)

In Latin countries tradition has suggested a different way of fitting an urban house to the land, as we have already seen in the plan of the house on Netzahualcoyotl Street in Cuernavaca. The house makes almost no gesture to the street; it merely abuts it with the blandest of faces. (14) Inside is the surprise as the house surrounds its lawn and garden of flowers and fruit trees. (15) A *mirador*, a small covered porch on the roof, is large enough for a hammock and a few chairs. Placed so as not to disturb the privacy of nearby patios, it gives a new dimension to the enclosed house on an urban lot by providing views to the cathedral, the plaza, and the distant mountains. Ascending to it from the gallery is a stair just arduous

11. *Main Street, Mendocino City, California*

12. *Chester Terrace, London, by John Nash, 1825*

195

13. *A house in Charleston, South Carolina, nineteenth century*

14. *A house in Cuernavaca, Mexico*

15. *Garden, a house in Cuernavaca*

16. Mirador, *a house in Cuernavaca*

enough to set the *mirador* off as a special place. (16)

An enormous advantage of surrounding, which can be seen in this house, is the ease with which the house can fit directly onto a street and tight up against other houses, so that all the open land on a small lot is where it counts, and can be seen from the house and used by the occupants. This eliminates the token front and side yards of American suburbia, which often serve only to give the owner exercise with a lawn mower.

Philip Johnson's house in Cambridge, Massachusetts, is a clear version of surrounding. Its blank wood garden walls surround the site, and make it a private realm to be seen only from inside. (17)

Suburban lots, often with required building setbacks of more than a third their depth, offer the fewest possibilities for variety in siting, a maddening fact when we consider that it is in the suburbs that most new houses are being built.

Merging is an obvious possibility if the site is thickly wooded, which in the case of many new developments it is not, at least after the developer's bulldozers have done their work. Surrounding the house with walls or high hedges, as in Santa Barbara, is also a possibility, if local tradition has sanctioned it; otherwise it may seen antisocial.

In most American towns, in fact, tradition has decreed that houses claim their sites, and the unsullied residential areas which remain here and there from the early part of this century are splendid, sociable manifestations of the tradition. (18) In them, houses were placed rather near the street and were connected to it and to the sidewalks by walkways from their front doors, which were actually used. Often these houses had front porches, from which the inhabitants could survey the passing scene.

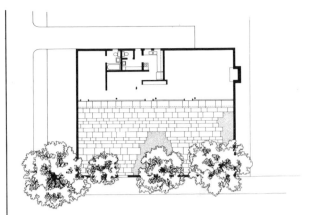

17. *Johnson house, Cambridge, Massachusetts, by Philip Johnson, 1942*

199

18. Elm Street, Lumberton, North Carolina, ca. 1910

Now most houses in towns are shoved back from the street, the sidewalks have been abandoned, and the porches removed. The front door has become an unconvincing symbol, useless because of the more immediate access to the back which the automobile allows. The result of all this readjustment is that all vestiges of human habitation have vanished from the façades of houses, and instead of claiming their front lawns, they blankly ignore them. The lawns become wasteful foregrounds for stage-set houses along streets void of everything but passing cars. (19)

In marked contrast is the complex web of human association that James Agee found on a street in Knoxville in 1915:

It has become that time of evening when people sit on their porches, rocking gently and talking gently and watching the street and the standing up into their sphere of possession of trees, of birds' hung havens, hangars. People go by; things go by. A horse, drawing a buggy, breaking his hollow iron music on the asphalt; a loud auto; a quiet auto; people in pairs, not in a hurry, scuffling, switching their weight of aestival body. talking casually. . . .

The four ways of fitting a house to the land—merging, claiming, enfronting, and surrounding—provide broad categories into which all the good houses we know can be classified. Often, though, a house will do several things at once as it sits on the land, and some memorable houses are combinations of more than one way of siting.

Mount Vernon, for example, enfronts the Potomac River on one side. But on the other a pair of curving arcades connect the house to outbuildings in a partial gesture of surrounding. (20) The scale of this side of the house, and of the arcades and the outbuildings, is smaller than that on the river

19. A contemporary suburban street

20. *Plantation front, Mount Vernon, Fairfax County, Virginia, 1785*

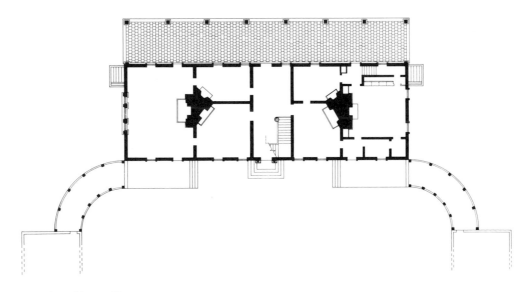

21. *Plan, Mount Vernon*

front, and what is created on this "planta-tion" side of the house is not unlike a village green, just as the activities that went on there once were those associated with the everyday life of the place, rather than with the ceremony which the river front suggests. It is interesting to note, too, that the way the rooms are assembled inside has nothing at all to do with the acts of enfronting or sur-rounding, for the plan is a simple and rather disorderly version of rooms bunched. (21)

Robert Adam's town house for Lord Derby, which we described as an example of rooms linked, managed to fit onto its land in two ways. Like the house on Netzahual-coyotl Street in Cuernavaca, it surrounded its urban site with the aid of a wall on one side, but unlike that house, it also enfronted its street and the square beyond.

In the condominium at the Sea Ranch there are three modes of siting: in the gently sloping shed roofs and the rough, unpainted redwood walls there is an element of merging with the meadow where the building is placed. But the strong shape of the building, punctuated by its tower, stakes a recogniz-able claim on the land. And as a group, the condominium units surround a courtyard and a parking compound.

The Smyth house, too, uses two ways of fitting itself to the land. Forced by legal constraint and a recognized obligation to its surburban neighborhood, it enfronts its blank front lawn, and then tries to counter this sterility, like a miniaturized version of Mount Vernon, by sprouting arcades and a garage on the sides and back to enclose a part of the site for the owners' private use.

Inflecting the scheme

Mapping

Once you have made your decisions, fitting the basic arrangement of rooms and machines on a piece of land in a way that connects with the structure of your dream world, there comes a further series of acts which add to the livability of your house. We are calling them *inflections* of the scheme, though no one word can summon to mind the great variety of these acts of habitation. There do seem to be two classes of inflection: those nuances found within the place and those added on. Architects earlier in the century made a strong distinction in favor of the former. "Ornament is crime," Adolf Loos declared, and Ludwig Mies van der Rohe called for "discovery, not invention." Our own attitude is more relaxed; there seem to us times when the one (discovery) is called for and times that require the other (invention), just as there are times when cooks season their food to reveal its natural flavor and times when they decide to supersede that natural flavor with something more palatable or more interesting.

We call the first process *mapping*, in which you describe to yourself (and thereby discover) where you are and what you are near. Windows and doors and paths and porches are major elements on this chart, as symbols for mountains and roads and bays and archipelagos are important on real maps. And the techniques of architects' mapping, like those of the cartographer, are of course based on emphasizing only features or relationships that seem important, and down-playing the rest.

The second process we call *collecting*, although it includes other devices as well for ornamenting and extending the claim you lay to a place. We make special note of the deployment of colors and textures, or collections of things, and of the pleasures of the temporary, which we enjoy in camping out, and of the small, which prompts the miniaturizing of things, from toy trains to dollhouses to parts of your house itself.

Mapping establishes the relationship between you and something you recognize. It helps you find out where you are, and it also helps describe the overall structure of the place you are in, making it comprehensible and therefore habitable.

Being inside, at the center of, on the edge

of, over, under, around the corner, beyond, or just next to something are basic acts of habitation. These acts we believe require that a house have many places, that there be enclosures, markers, and other elements to map complex personal domains.

To imagine how full a place your house might be, visualize the maps of locations that you love. Consider the number of different things that they record: landmarks and routes, harbors, forests, mountains, parks, campgrounds, and scenic outlooks. Consider, too, the elements with which you especially remember a place, and chart your course—tree-shaded roads, buildings standing clear in the memory, distant views across marshes or rolling hills, a surprising sign, or spots of cherished associations. All these are like the range of conditions that can exist, too, in the inner landscape of your house.

Rooms provide the general terrain, and some of the machines within them can develop into landmarks or way stations. In carelessly made houses there will be nothing more, save the disorderly routes blazed between doors, or stifling corridors—the unseemly domestic equivalents of freeways that sever more than they connect.

The topography of the house can and should contain much more. Windows, for instance, can be shaped to make special places to sit midway between inside and out. Doors can be located so that they stage views through the rooms of the house or invite a dramatic entry. Light can flood through the rooms or be pocketed in special places. Changes of level can provide differing vantage points in the same rooms and differentiate between uses. The structure of the house itself, its roof, walls, and columns, can serve to delineate locations and relate them to the map of the whole. Most directly, the house can have special places inside,

fireplaces or aedicular shelters, for example, that serve as symbolic centers, as psychic landmarks from which to gauge one's position.

Children constantly make places in miniature, remapping the house by playing house. Tables and chairs and blanket tents strung between them create a diminutive realm for the imagination, smaller than the room the children are in, but offering wider scope to their fantasies.

Our Koizim house is like an aedicular village. (1) It was conceived as a house made of many little houses, all gathered under a large hipped roof. (2) Rough white stucco walls enclose distinct places to dwell, in front of and behind the fire, by a bar near the dining area, or in separate chambers for sleeping. Between these little houses are high irregular spaces, thought of as enclosed porches. (3) In this case the empty stages are the space left between tightly knit rooms inside the little houses. From the vantage point of the aedicular shelters the larger rooms are "outside." These outside rooms are indoors, but they are more public than the rest, imaginable as a "plaza" for the aedicular village.

The distinction between inner and outer rooms is sustained in many details of the house. Windows facing the terrace in this "outside" room are continuous, with an outdoor truss serving as a kind of overhang to help protect against the southern sun. (4) The truss above eye level marks a space midway between outdoors and in, merging the two. The segments of this wall that are solid are painted with patterns that diminish their solidity. (5) Windows and walls of rooms in the little plaster houses, however, are treated in an opposite manner. Each window in the thick white wall is a special event, each opening is a frame, a place to notice and perhaps to stand in, a sharp edge

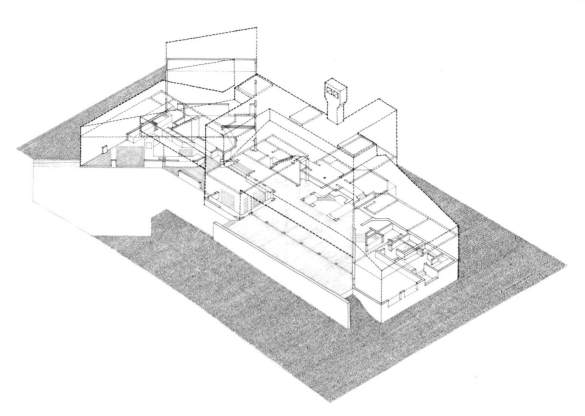

1. Koizim house, Westport, Connecticut, by MLTW/Moore–Turnbull, 1969

2. Exterior, Koizim house

3. Living room, Koizim house

4. Exterior showing kitchen corner, Koizim house

between inside and out. In the kitchen is a deliberate exception. Here the pattern is contradicted by two great sheets of glass that dissolve the kitchen's triangular corner into a sunny breakfast place merging with the terrace.

Windows

Windows do more than let in light and air. The way they are placed in a wall affects our understanding of the whole house, confirming and helping give point to the established order or denying and adjusting it when there is cause.

Examples of the multiple uses of windows in architecture are, of course, legion. The pattern of openings in a wall is an important part of most architectural styles. In mapping a house, however, the window shapes and frames play a far more subtle and important role than just that of making patterns on its face. For example, the bay window, in its many guises, carries a suggestion of personal enclosure. Whether bulbous or rectangular, skewed on the corner or centered on the façade, bracketed from below or capped by a tower on the top, it is a building detail that acknowledges the presence of people. It becomes as much a place to be seen in as a place to look out from.

Windows can imply a great deal, both by their shape and by their position. The main window in the second floor of the house Robert Venturi designed for his mother is a case in point. Its oversize arch sweeping down to the floor would, by classical conventions, belong to the façade of a much larger building. From the inside, though, it suggests to its occupant, we suspect, residence in the attic of a Roman villa. (6)

Still another case is a comparison of two walls that are each made almost entirely of glass. Maynard Lyndon's house in Malibu and Philip Johnson's glass house in New

5. Interior looking toward the water, Koizim house

6. Upper bedroom, Venturi house, Chestnut Hill, Pennsylvania, by Venturi and Rauch, 1962

211

7. Glass wall, Lyndon house, Malibu, California, by Maynard Lyndon, 1949

Canaan have in common their date of construction and their use of full sheets of glass stretching from floor to ceiling. In other respects, however, they are quite unlike. The house in Southern California bends every effort to merge indoors and out. Johnson's, bracing itself for the more demanding New England weather and suffused with a stricter classicism, separates indoors and out even while the walls are fully transparent. The difference in approach is apparent in the way the windows are made and how they are joined to other surfaces. Together these details provide clues to the owner's point of view about how the window is used, and what it can say.

The glass of the Lyndon house is set either into large aluminum frames that slide aside or directly into the concrete foundation and roof of the house. (7) From the inside the glass appears to enter the ground at the bottom and the plane of the ceiling at the top. Vertical frames are infrequent, thin, and inconspicuous. Pipe columns to hold up the roof are irregularly spaced and painted in soft colors to minimize their presence. There is no evident limit to the enclosure. The space continues uninterrupted across the terrace to the parapet at the edge of the sea.

Philip Johnson's glass walls, on the other hand, are framed with black steel in shapes carefully proportioned and meant to be appreciated (discreetly) as pattern. (8) The edges of the glass and of the house are precise and measured, ticked off by frames of steel. The majority of the glass is fixed; there are no disappearing sliding walls, only a single door in the middle of each wall opening onto narrow stone steps. Here the doors mark the transition from inside to out and map clearly the limits of the house. They even, by their location, reinforce symmetries which reveal the classical antecedents of the design.

212

8. *Glass wall, Johnson house, New Canaan, Connecticut, by Philip Johnson, 1949*

9. Inglenook, Koizim house, Westport,
Connecticut, by MLTW/Moore–Turnbull

10. Exterior, Koizim house

Paths and entries

In the Koizim house, doorways are related to
an axial path that cuts through the elements
of the house. The path leads from a court
at the front door to the entry of the little
house holding the master bedroom and bath
at the other end. A parallel passage on an
upper level connects the white blocks of
this mini-village with doorways to private
bedrooms spaced along its sides. The passage
is not uninterrupted. The white walls of the
fireplace nook stand in the way, although
openings in the walls allow the mind's eye
to continue along the axial path while the
body detours.

This interrupting space is an inglenook, an
oversized hearth, shaped like a room. Since
it interrupts the passage, it claims attention.
It is the most clearly visible object in the
aedicular village, and with its high façade (9)
it enfronts the "almost outdoors" space like
a church or public building might face a
Mexican village square. It is joined to the
large room it enfronts by a small stoop
raised a step from the general level. Given its
large hearth with a fire to sit by, it is the
evident center of comfort and enclosure in
the house.

The front entry court, from which the
axial passage had proceeded, is lodged
between the mini-buildings that house the
kitchen, an extra bedroom, and the garage.
Their shapes are constrained by their need to
fit under the big hip roof. The front wall of
the court has large high openings that step
up as they approach the door, leaving no
doubt that this is the major entry. (10)

Doors

For houses that are lived in with any degree
of ceremony, the major entry has to be clear.
Front doors and their surroundings are
important landmarks for visitors. The lavish
attention that has been spent on entry places

in all forms of architecture attests to the importance of the territorial distinction between inside and out. The point of transition between the two has persistently been used as a spot where information is conveyed about the building and its purpose. In medieval religious buildings in both Europe and Asia, elaborately carved figures generally guard doorways and bespeak the virtues and the terrors of right-doing and wrong as you enter the house of the Lord. In the twentieth-century pilgrimage church at Ronchamp, Le Corbusier made the ceremonial entry special by setting a huge door on pivots and covering it with an enameled symbolic painting, which makes it altogether unlike ordinary doors that open and close on daily lives. (11)

At Gunston Hall the front door is set in a porch (a little house) and surrounded on the sides and above by windows that open the vestibule to the daylight outside. (12) Inside, doors into each of the principal rooms are detailed with exceptional care and set into the thick wall to form vestibules that mark the act of passing from one room to another, mapping domains for a life that was circumscribed by traditions.

Our own lives are not likely to be so neatly circumscribed, yet the doors that link rooms together, or shut them off, influence our understanding of a house and its use. The mapping that doors impose on a house is pervasive, yet sometimes so subtle that it goes unnoticed. But each door implies a path, requires an action, and either shuts away a segment of your domestic life or opens it to view, to hearing, and to smell, and sometimes to the outdoors.

Adjacent rooms can be joined in a variety of ways. Sliding doors may open them freely to each other, or carefully spaced openings may emphasize their distinction and determine precisely the paths between them.

11. Doorway, Notre Dame du Haut, Ronchamp, France, by Le Corbusier, 1955

12. Entrance, Gunston Hall, Fairfax County, Virginia, 1758

Doors standing open or doors shut serve as vivid social signals. They can help the inhabitants of a house alter its map to suit their mood or the demands on their time, inviting sociability or indicating the need to be alone. Often the simple choice between open and closed is not sufficiently subtle to serve these needs, and arrangements that offer more choice are in order: double doors with vestibules, Dutch doors that open separately on the top, or doors with windows in them.

Studies of a dormitory at the University of California at Berkeley provide an example where the simple choice was not enough. If the students' doors were open, they were beleaguered with visitors and unable to work. If, on the other hand, they closed their doors, this was often taken as a sign that they were unfriendly or hostile. At Oxford, over centuries, more complicated communication has grown up. The rooms were fitted, originally for purposes of coping with winter weather, with two doors, an outer and an inner. If the inner door is closed, but the other not, there is a clear message that the inhabitant is busy, but will receive visitors. When the outer door is closed, however ("sporting the oak," it is called), the occupant is not in or is not to be disturbed. A psychiatrist friend of ours has developed a similar code for his office, using a pull shade on the glass window in his door to indicate to passersby in the corridor whether he can receive visitors or is engaged in consultation. When the shade is pulled down, interruption is unwarranted.

Because of the symbolic nature of doors, they can develop ambiguity as well as privacy and sociability. Long casual conversations will often be held in doorways when neither party is prepared to commit himself to entering or leaving the room and thereby formalizing or ending a discussion. This is often true, too, of departing guests and unexpected visitors.

Porches and in-between realms

Porches provide further lingering places, extending the in-between realms into the out-of-doors. As a protected place for entering and leaving a house, the front porch, as James Agee described it, has traditionally been of great importance in mapping, indicating the character of a house and determining its relations to the street of which it might be a part. Of late, of course, the front porch has become a casualty of air conditioning and busier streets. In most places its uses have withered, so cost-cutting builders have generally dismissed porches from the vernacular of residential building. Even now, however, entries may evoke poignant recollections since, like the one at Gunston Hall, they can so neatly become little aedicular houses.

The place of the house in its surroundings is strongly colored by the way that rooms inside meet the shared space outside. When the land itself has many levels this meeting can become quite complex. Sometimes, especially when the site is small and the uses demanded of it are numerous, all of it may need to be considered (as in the house in Cuernavaca) as an assembly of rooms indoors and out, enclosed, sheltered and shaded by landscaping as well as building. When the site is larger or wilder, gradations from controlled to uncontrolled will probably be indicated, as in Philip Johnson's houses in New Canaan.

In Edgartown and Santa Barbara we noted still other patterns for mapping the private terrain outdoors. Picket fences, in the former, map out the boundaries of the land without enclosing it much, where in the latter all space is characteristically surrounded by hedges and walls.

Other realms between outdoors and in are also vivid agents for describing the shape and character of the whole house. Bay windows, porches (13), sheltering eaves, pergolas, terraces with ledges at their boundaries, skylit rooms or atria inside, as well as walled courts, greenhouses, solaria, or yards fenced by hedges are examples of these in-between realms. In each case they modify one or two of the three elements of enclosure—floor, walls, and roof—as they make transparent the top or sides and sometimes change the surface underfoot.

Some of these structures reach out into the surroundings, claiming the outdoors as private space. Others, like porches and terraces, can make a place for the individual in a shared realm to which the outside has been admitted, and in turn provide that realm with stages for neighborly transaction, or at least box seats for the passing show. Some, like atria or walled gardens, swallow the outdoors and bring it wholly within the private world.

Whether you desire shade or sun, shelter from the wind or openings to the view and passing breezes, exposure or privacy, will depend on the climate of the place and will be influenced as well by local norms of hospitality and seclusion. The exact location of these in-between realms must be considered, too, so you get their mediation between inside and out when you want it, and direct juxtaposition of indoors and out (as in an unimpeded view) when you want that.

Landmarks

Geometry is often used to give related shapes to rooms and machine realms so that they can be easily mapped. The recurrence of a given set of shapes or proportional relations provides assurance that the place is an orderly whole. It can thus help to

13. Skylit room, Tempchin house, Bethesda, Maryland, by MLTW/Moore–Turnbull and Rurik Ekstrom, 1967

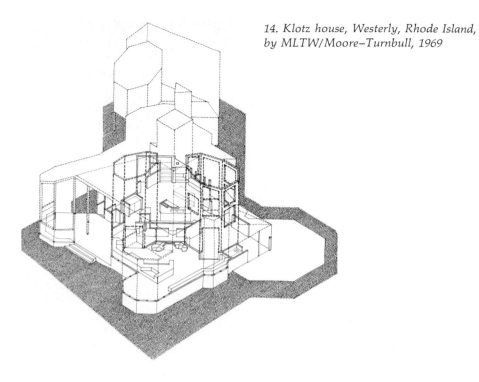

14. Klotz house, Westerly, Rhode Island, by MLTW/Moore–Turnbull, 1969

15. Exterior, Klotz house

establish a hierarchy of importances for locations within the house. Architects in the last several decades, however, have often been tyrannically geometrical, mapping houses with shapes that deliberately eschew associations beyond themselves. Frank Lloyd Wright's houses planned on a hexagonal grid (so only hexagonal beds will fit) or the rash of houses built as clusters of identical pavilions, where every room or machine domain had to be the same size and shape as every other, are cases in point. We believe, on the other hand, that a house built around recognizable *landmarks* associated directly with human use will generally be more satisfying than one that depends on the imposition of an abstract, totally consistent geometry.

The Klotz house is mapped by a cluster of tall spaces that serve as landmarks at its center and a roof that falls away from them in all directions. (14–15) At the core of the house are two hollow octagonal spaces that reach from the floor to the apex of the roof. They are landmarks which give comprehensible position to the rest of the rooms in the house, since the edges of the house and particular rooms inside take their shape from the exigencies of location and use. One towering hollow space is the point of entry. The other, down a few steps and flooded with light from above, is used for formal dining. (16) Between the two a narrow stair passage squeezes past an exposed chimney that twists assertively into the peak. (17) Stairs climb past and around these landmarks to the master bedroom and study, both of them open to the high spaces. Places to cook, to eat more casually, and for children to sleep trail off to one side of the pair of landmarks at the core. On the opposite side of these spaces and up a few steps is a low, thickly carpeted sitting room in which the landmark chimney becomes

16. *Dining tower, Klotz house*

17. *Stairs seen from dining area, Klotz house*

219

18. Fireplace, Klotz house

rock, with giant boulders disposed around the fire. (18) As the obverse face of the smooth-surfaced core, this room with its rough hearth and the shaggy carpet extending up the walls even into bookcases is another world.

From outside, the house hangs closely onto the hill it surmounts. While clearly claiming its site, it is also akin to it, its bulk sloping as the hill does, its edges eroded by sheltered passages and quarried to let light into specific places. On the entry side the roof extends out to form a porch which repeats the high octagonal spaces of the inner landmarks.

Remapping

Just as mapping is an aid to making sense of a new house, remapping can make altogether new sense of an existing house. Even if an already determined assembly of rooms is given, it can be drastically remapped by changing the openings between the rooms making new paths through rooms already there and altering their use as well as their apparent form.

In a house in Cambridge, Massachusetts, such alterations went one step further: the entire path structure of the house was remapped, cutting off some rooms into separate apartments and cutting an open core at the center into which the remaining rooms upstairs and down now open. (19) The jagged rotunda opening off the front door is painted in brilliant colors and struck by pigmented lighting to map it as the central and extraordinary landmark for the existing assembly of perimeter rooms. (20)

A new bay has been added and the rear wall of the house now consists of glass doors sliding open to a terrace. The remainder of the wall that was removed now sports a false arch with lights embedded in it to mark the place for a dining table. (21)

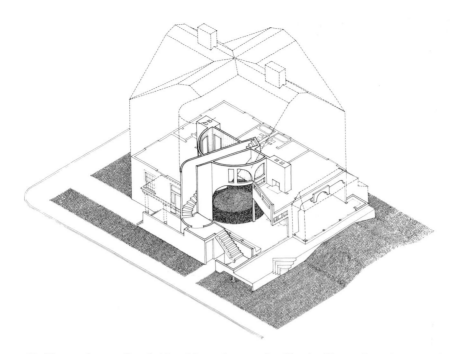

19. Murray house, Cambridge, Massachusetts, by Charles Moore Associates, 1973

20. Rotunda, Murray house

Except for the added bay and large windows placed beside it (both at the fenced rear of the house and therefore invisible from the street) there are no substantial changes in the exterior shell. The outside appearance remains that of a characteristic turn-of-the-century Cambridge wood house. At some future date its entry porch is due for remapping too, to hint at what lies inside.

Exploring

Many pleasures of a house come from exploring it, from learning how to recognize and use the places it includes. Your house can be a rich field for exploration if you attend to the juxtaposition of qualities, pitting rough and smooth, high and low, open and closed against each other to make small places within and provide a sequence of them through the house.

Combining contrasting vistas with a calculated choreography of movement in the house can make experiencing it especially vivid. Platforms, stairs, and other changes of level are particularly potent, since they both engage the body in maneuvering them and alter your point of view, enlarging the outlook as your eye rises above obstructions or increasing enclosure and connection with the ground as you go down.

Up and down, right and left, front and back are not for human beings identical, as they are for the six faces of a cube. That seems evident enough, except that the rigid geometries which surface in nineteenth-century city plans and twentieth-century office buildings so commonly deny these differences that we may begin to think it is people who misunderstand the grid, rather than noting that it is the undifferentiated grid which is inadequate for human expression. Front is the opposite of back, not interchangeable with it. Up and down have

21. *Dining area, Murray house*

223

always had opposite importance, whether they refer to deities or trips on drugs. Attics and cellars have opposite psychic as well as geographic connotations, and even terms like "dextrous" and "sinister" come from a world that has never been symmetrical from right to left. All these qualities, and gravity, and the movement of the sun in the sky, and of people on their feet, and the strictures of human use and memory create, within the framework of rooms and machines and dreams, an incredibly rich and complex world of experiences. To make sense of that, to find the sequences and orders that matter to you, to draw order from the bewilderment and strength from the richness is the object of the discovering and sorting process of mapping.

Collecting

There can come a time when discovering, clarifying, and mapping a house are not enough. Then adding on—embroidering, ornamenting—is a possibility. It is a possibility, as we have noted, that was angrily excluded by many Modern architects who insisted that lilies were not for gilding. To us, this adding on seems as natural as it is common in everyday practice. Children claim walls by drawing on them, and they control the territory of their rooms by spreading about their toys, dolls, and other possessions. College students less often draw on the walls, but they continue to take possession with books and clothes strewn to the edges of their domain. Adults act similarly, claiming the space of their house with ornamental chairs, tables, and plants instead of toys, and affixing someone else's painting to the wall rather than drawing there themselves. A similar addition may occur if the occupant uses objects and their locations, and colors, textures, and materials to establish a milieu that can be recognized as his own. The power of these additions to adjust the whole place is evident in a passage from a book by Ronald Blythe, describing a small house in Akenfield, consisting of two rooms linked:

> The cottage is partly a soldier's resettlement hut of the First World War and partly a railway carriage, and is quite inordinately pretty. The two units are set in an "L" and the joint is covered with house-leeks and stone-crop, cushions of grass and Paul Scarlet roses. Brass carriage handles glitter behind leaves. Little paths maze around and are edged with beer bottles, their necks driven into the earth. It is a toy house for playing mothers-and-fathers in. Except that the fathers, big, clumsy, nasty things, have long since been ousted from the game. Their speckled photographs glare down from the walls.

Color too is an extension of the qualities of a place, adding to the brightness of a room or, in the case of dark colors, absorbing its light. Color has its own set of connotations, and the decision to paint a room one color or another can substantially alter its character. The white walls of many modern houses were, one presumes, uncolored in order that they might avoid the added-on connotations which colors bring. Those connotations are not simple.

Color, it seems to us, is like proportion; though there are endless and often conflicting rules for its use, its chief characteristic is that it says something to people, based chiefly on their recollections of previous experiences. Some people really like lavender; others are offended by it. People generally agree that some colors feel cool (like blue or green) while others feel hot (like red or orange). Some colors seem cheerful (lemon-yellow, for instance) and dark colors may feel cozy, which can induce a sense of well-being, itself cheerful. Connotations of colors may have the effect of heightening their inherent qualities or masking them. Contrast of unlike hues (the actual color), or values (how light or dark), or intensities (how bright or gray) can create dramatic effect. Continuity of like colors or values or intensities can reinforce each other; a random assortment of colors may simply confuse or mask each one's effect. Individual colors, or particular groups of colors, may recall something special to some (hot Mexican colors, or the colors of Monet's water lilies, or Etruscan colors) and be liked or disliked for that.

Materials as well have connotations composed of their color and their texture: the dark board and shingles of summer cottages in the North Woods; the silvery-grayed boards of beach houses; the white stucco of the Mediterranean seaside. Their roughness or their smoothness, their pattern, their warmth or feeling of cool allow materials to represent images that we cherish or that we seek.

The natural colors and the fragility of materials in Japanese rooms, for instance, set up a specific stage for living that has been highly admired for its coherence and economy of means. It is evident, however, that there are patterns of behavior that such rooms will not accept, and in traditional Japanese houses with no chairs, certain gestures and postures are in fact demanded. There is implicit within the space and serenity and delicate patterns that we admire in Japanese houses a claim on our behavior inside them that is difficult for most Westerners (and some modern Japanese) to endure.

Of more recent and local derivation has been the use of paint to make patterns that are independent of the basic structure of the room, changing its apparent size and shape, joining places that are separate or seeming to set asunder walls that are one. (1) Paint and coloring may be used in several ways to reinforce as well as contradict the patterns in the house. The colors may constitute a system of coding, as they do when they identify the components of the house, differentiating structural members, trim pieces, panels, ducts, and pipes from each other and from the enclosing and partitioning walls. The different natural qualities of materials may provide similar enrichment, as when woods of different grains and colors are used together and their patterns celebrated. As elucidation of the building's structure and the processes which created it, this use of color and grain can carry complex information. By setting before our minds a collection of facts, it infuses the place with evidence of the human acts of building.

There may, however, be other characteristics of a house that interest you more than the way it was built, or you may wish to surround yourself with images and materials that have nothing to do with building. You may be fascinated by antique silver, or by chessmen, or by the collection of toy soldiers or ships in bottles. By surrounding yourself with things that have special meaning for you, which you have chosen from among other similar things and about which you know a great deal, you can add dimension

1. Dining area, Taylor Town Houses, Norwalk, Connecticut, by Charles Moore Associates, 1973

2. Living room, Moore house, Centerbrook, Connecticut, by Charles Moore, 1971

to the place you inhabit and to its capacity
to nurture your imagination. Whether they
are collections of chairs, rocks, engravings,
toys, or (more usually) books, they gain
their power from the act of discrimination
and commitment that they represent and
from the investment of care and knowledge
that attends them. They are worthless if they
are not personal. (2)

The display of collections makes them a
part of the house. Setting the objects of your
attention into some concentrated place and
in an order that provokes comparison and
discrimination allows others to share in your
enthusiasms. Pictures completely covering a
wall or shelves of books are collections that
extend your own involvement with the
house. Photographs, drawings, or pieces of
ornament from old buildings can make
vivid your recollections of other places and
add their overtones to the house you are in.
You may even wish to build the house itself
of found parts, making it out of old
windows and used lumber (3) or shiny new
industrial components clipped together.
Almost any way will add meaning to your
house, if the way you have chosen has
meaning for you.

Establishing limits, once again, is necessary
to the idea of collections. It is not possible
for you to have all the books or all the
pictures that you might want, so you must
choose to have some and forgo others.
The very act of choosing is a creative act.

Sir John Soane, in his house in London,
amassed an extraordinary collection of
artifacts and art that became an integral part
of the place, so richly interlayered that in his
later years Soane himself published a book
describing the house. In 1833, his eightieth
year, he made arrangements for the house
to be established as a museum, and he
formed an endowment for its support. (4–5)

The house and its collection are insepa-

3. Smith house, Harvard, Massachusetts, by
Maurice Smith, 1974

4. Soane house, London, by Sir John Soane, 1812–34

5. Plan, Soane house

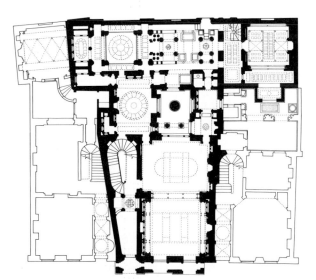

rable. The conventional rooms are filled with paintings and objects that bespeak the romantic classicism that characterized Soane's work as an architect. Thoroughly steeped in classical traditions and in the rules attending them, he yet disposed objects and molded spaces with a disciplined abandon that was wholly original. His was a collector's passion, delighting in the juxtaposition and aggregation of meaning, as in the mysterious effects of light and shadow; it was a passion too strong to be constrained by conventional precedent or regular arrangements of space.

As his collection grew, Soane had purchased two houses adjoining his row house and eventually rebuilt them, filling the back of all three with curious exhibition spaces replete with multiple views and illusionistic devices. These picturesque rooms had especially romantic names in the basement which housed Catacomb, Crypt, Sepulchral Chamber, Monument Court, and Monk's Parlour. Arranged over the walls of these rooms and the ones above and projecting into them is a staggering array of Classical, Renaissance, and Neoclassical urns, sculpture, column capitals, friezes, and sphinxes, not to mention a mummy case, skeleton, and fragments of other architectural details carved in stone or cast in plaster. (6)

So that he might house many of his favored paintings in the small, first-floor Picture-Room, Soane devised the arrangement we have already mentioned of hinged panels that swing out from the wall to reveal additional layers of paintings behind and finally, on one side, a view into a recess filled with sculpture and more paintings. This recess adjoins onto the Monk's Parlour below, a place of altogether different character, with medieval objects, and an outlook to the tiny Monk's Yard, where Soane noted, "The ruins of a monastery arrest the

6. *Museum, Soane house*

231

7. *Dining room from the library, Soane house*

attention." Similar illusionism in a chastened form is employed in the library and dining room. (7) A single space was remodeled from two rooms of the previous house and is divided still by a complicated dropped arch, its edges disembodied in a flurry of recesses and spindles. Busts high in the corners of the room turn to gaze into spherical mirrors that reflect the full room in compressed and distorted form. (8) On the ceiling are paintings commissioned by Soane of Phoebus in his car, preceded by Aurora and the Morning Star, led on by the Hours, etc.

Far smaller, but even more astounding and marvelous, however, is the Breakfast Parlour (9) which manages, in its tiny compass, to sport a spherical ceiling springing from four segmented arches supported in their turn by four pilasters, forming, as Soane noted, "a rich canopy." All the critical places are covered with mirrors, save a sky-lit lantern at the top of the little dome, on which are "Scriptural subjects" in painted glass. Light bathes the walls of the room from skylights behind the vaulted part of the ceiling, and views from this strategically located little space reveal the Monument Court and the Museum, as well as the living rooms.

Soane wrote that "the arrangement and decoration present a succession of those fanciful effects which constitute the poetry of architecture." They serve, too, as a particularly rich illustration of our suggestion to keep the myth up off the floor. The complex subdivisions overhead, made magic by the mirrors, along with the illusion of depth in the tiny pictures, contribute to this room, seeming at once minuscule and cosmic. Soane's poignant exaltation of the almost trivial is peerless, beyond any hope of emulation. For most of the rest of us, a more relaxed assemblage will have to suffice.

Something as simple as spices for cooking,

8. *Arch between dining room and library, Soane house*

9. Breakfast Parlour, Soane house

if you especially care for them, may become a collection, stored in a variety of vessels, sorted for use, labeled boldly, and arranged on narrow shelves for display. (10) The game is lost if you buy the set, shelves and all, prepackaged in the supermarket. If you are really an herb freak, and live in a suitable climate, you will wish to extend your claim to the out-of-doors, cultivating there an herb garden filled with diminutive plants like those represented in medieval garden paintings.

Specialized gardens are an especially important form of collecting; terraces and patios and hedge-trimmed lawns extend a claim on the place where you live, and planting a tree, like hoisting a flag, can be a simple means for staking a claim on your land. All these additions offer the benefits of defining your place with things that live. Their growth over time, the changes that come with seasons, even the rituals of care and nourishment that growing things demand introduce additional levels of meaning and value to your house.

Over time, landscaping can fully transform the character of a place. Early photographs of Maynard Lyndon's house at Malibu (whose windows we have looked at), built on a treeless and grassy plain, contrast strikingly with its appearance more than twenty years later, sheltered by trees, enclosed by hedges, and adorned with luxuriant plants. (11–12) When the house was built, its design was based in large measure on assuring for its occupants uninterrupted views of the ocean. Planting areas in front of the full-glass walls and bedrooms and baths ensured that they could be curtained with live bamboo and that the foreground to the view would be soft. As the site developed into a series of outdoor rooms laced by shadowing trees and subdivided by hedges and shrubs

10. Shelves for spices

11. Lyndon house, Malibu, California, by Maynard Lyndon, 1949

12. Lyndon house in 1972

(and as the brown smudge of Los Angeles smog advanced across the horizon), the sweeping view diminished in importance, and pine and eucalyptus trees have been planted in front to reduce exposure to the sea and to shade the terrace from sun and glare. The collecting and nurturing care that have been invested there have given form to a landscape that now has a life of its own. The house, in its spareness and transparency, is rather like a tent, a permanent camp in a site that has been cultivated around it.

There is a special fascination for the independence that camping out in a more conventional cloth tent involves: the close-fitting little house (the tent), and ingeniously packed cooking utensils, the freedom of movement have a share in the fascination of apparent self-sufficiency in an external world of someone else's making, with associations all the way from pioneers to astronauts.

Camping out may take place in buildings as well as landscapes, especially when the rooms of a place no longer fit its users or were fashioned to the impulses of another time. Italian architects, after the Second World War, found themselves often confronted by the need to transform large palaces to other uses. Their response, constrained by limited means and by respect for the traditions and artistry embodied in the rooms of these buildings, was often to design an elegant form of camping out, laying claim to the place with furniture, collections, and minimal partitioning rather than altering the basic nature of the rooms. A quarter-century later, saturated with gloom by their visions of environmental decline, Italian designers are still exhibiting various transformations of camping out— sealed capsules that unfold into neutral surroundings or disassemble into components for staking out a claim indoors or out.

The impulses based on camping out, or

portability, have, of course, far wider implications in the burgeoning mobile home industry, where more importance can probably be attached to the image of mobility and freedom than the actual promise of it. But the opposite desire, too, has some power: Our Champy house project on a New Hampshire beach is in response to the desire of a young man, not yet married, to fix a place for generations, more like the family beach houses of the late nineteenth century than the "camps" of the Italian designers. (13) In sight of the sea, but approached from the woods, so the ocean view is withheld, the house is mapped with great complexity, but with powerful land-marks to give coherence: a tower containing a study with an open deck on top, and a high, wide hall that becomes the spine of the house. In the hall is an enormous wall, whose size and regularity give it special importance, making it a figurative backrest for looking out to sea. A few skylights spaced regularly above it allow streaks of sunlight to move across its surface. Falling across beams and columns and into recesses, they will inhabit the space even before a family will, with shifting pools of light and shadow.

The catwalks and stairs, nooks and bays set out territory for exploration and discovery in the near future. The more distant future is more loosely mapped, but the claim is already extended to it by concrete walls surrounding a parking court, meant as foundation for an ocean-front addition which can respond to the fancies of a yet unenvisaged moment. Meanwhile the limits are set, the opportunity is open, and James Champy can learn from the first steps of his house how to extend it. Just contemplating the splendid futures for these foundations may be adequate for years to come.

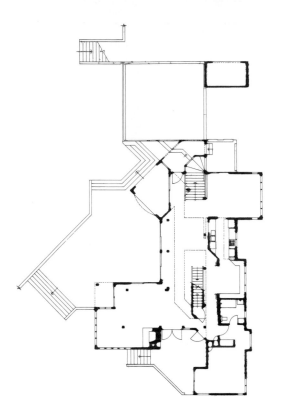

13. Champy house, Rye Beach, New Hampshire, by MLTW/Lyndon, 1973

The relaxed recollection of house past or future or house eternal comes much more often in the images of "little houses" that abound in the built world, in gabled porches, pedimented windows, in toy houses, and in the four-posted aediculas by which we set so much store. As architects we have enjoyed making such little houses inside as well as out, setting out for the inhabitants the same places for intensified habitation that were provided for saintly statues or the anointed in niches or on vaulted thrones in the ceremonial past, making places especially "inside" which might allow some part of the mind to play house more freely than it might otherwise do, to add little house to house, to gild, we suppose, the lily, and embroider the claim of the inhabitants on a place that is special to them.

Yours

Yours

Now it is time to establish a kind of check list to identify the choices which you must make if you are to invest your house with the care which will bring it alive as the center of your world.

There are many excellent books which describe in detail the techniques for building a house and keeping it strong and weather-tight, and we shall not attempt to repeat those descriptions here. Instead, we will describe only those choices which require a value judgment from you.

Care is the natural enemy of stereotype, and stereotype of care. So we must make whatever detours are necessary to avoid even such stereotypes as "living room," lest somebody ask, "What do you *do* there?" and you find yourself having to say, "Live."

To identify the components of your house, the facts which restrict or aid choice, the choices you actually have, their importance to you, and their intersection with other choices, we have organized the lists to follow certain paths. These are the paths made through your house by water, air, paper, food, dishes, clothing and linen, electricity, cars, and other objects. Then we list the paths made (and departed from) by adults and children in your household, by others you invite, by service people, by burglars, by pets. Finally, we describe the paths along which the mind and the mind's eye are enticed. Each of the paths can be labeled, and their intersections noted.

The answers you make will not define a "plan" for your house. They will serve instead as a test to check against the ways there are of assembling rooms and machine domains and fitting them to the site. Inevitably there will be conflicts, which you can resolve in favor of whatever is more important to you. There will also be ambiguities, which you can cherish if you are of a mind to. But don't cheat on the choices, or take shortcuts. The fruit of shortcuts is stereotype.

The paths of things and of people and of the mind's eye, then, we shall list as:
Water
Air
Paper
Food
Dishes and other cooking utensils
Clothing and linen

Electricity
Dirt
Cars
Other Objects
Adults (you should note them separately)
Children (you should note them separately)
Invited guests
Service people
The uninvited
Pets
Images

The first lists include, after a description of each element, a set of choices *(in italics)* with room for you to check your decision and to note its importance to you. With most of the choices we note the difficulties, limits, special opportunities, standard equipment, or standard dimensions relevant to that choice.

Water
Water falls onto your house from the sky, and drains away on or under the ground. It also enters in pipes and bottles, is used up or mixed with pollutants, and is then swept away. You're in for the falling water, unless you live in an apartment or a desert, and if you are within the reach of sanitary inspectors, you are in for piped water, too. The bottled is optional.

Not optional is the gravity which will cause the water to run inexorably downhill, or the changes water will cause in almost any material it touches, from silver-gray weathering and warping and staining and causing fungus on wood, to streaks on stucco and concrete, to rust on iron, to corrosion on aluminum, to the beautiful green patina on copper. Thus, decisions have to be made about every surface along the water's path, so that it can be impervious (like glass, marble, glazed tile, or Formica) or even changed for the better (like copper)

or be worth the continuing trouble (as some say oiled wood or a butcher block is).

How will the water from the sky get off the roof?

☐ *Uncontrolled*   This is the cheapest, but may be forbidden by local building codes, and it can mess up the garden or splatter against the foundation of the house.
☐ *Through gutters and downspouts*   They are relatively expensive and can clog with leaves or look bad.
☐ *Through spouts or gargoyles*   These can look fine, but might splash onto some vulnerable surface.

What do you want to do with the water when it hits the ground?

☐ *Let it soak in*   Okay if the soil is gravelly or sandy enough to absorb it.
☐ *Get rid of it underground*   Like gutters and downspouts, this method can be expensive.
☐ *Run it in visible channels*   Can be handsome and, if it fits your garden scheme, can take water to plants.

Where will your household water come from?

☐ *A well*   Necessary in the country and usually available.
☐ *A tank*   Necessary in the country where a well cannot be dug.
☐ *The city's pipes*   Always available in town and cheaper than a well or tank.

How will you heat some of it?

☐ *Oil*
☐ *Gas*
☐ *Electricity*
☐ *Other*   The answer to this set of choices, if it depends on cost, can be obtained by contacting each utility supplier.

Where will the heater be and how many of them?

☐ *Near the machines it serves*   This is the cheap-

est and most efficient, but won't work if all the
machines aren't close together.
- □ *One, serving machines spread apart* Less convenient since taps will take longer to warm up,
but more economical.
- □ *Several, serving separate groups of machines*
More convenient; less economical.

Where do you want water outside?

- □ *Near plants that need watering* Garden hoses
are cheapest; underground and automated
systems are available.
- □ *To form a pool or pond*

Inside, what do you want to wash your food in?

- □ *Single or double sink, of porcelain or stainless
steel* Sinks are usually mounted in counters;
the standard counter height is 36", but if you
are tall or short you may want to vary this.
Standard counter depth is 25".

What do you want to wash your dishes in?

- □ *The sink* Economical; tolerably convenient.
- □ *A dishwasher* This can be built under a
counter beside the sink, with a front opening—
in which case you will face the issue of
whether it should be right or left of the sink
—or in a portable machine which hooks to
the sink's water supply and generally opens
from the top.

Where do you want to wash your food and
dishes?

- □ *In a secluded area* Offers privacy and insulation for the rest of the house, from the noise
of your dishwasher if you have one. It also
offers you privacy, if you want it, from other
adults and children.
- □ *In a more open area adjoining a room or an
outdoor space* Depends on whether or not
you have someone else wash your food and
on whether or not you like to be with others
if you do it yourself.
- □ *With a view, whether from an open or a
secluded area* Can be pleasant and useful
for keeping an eye on your family.

Where do you like to mix drinks?

- □ *By the sink*
- □ *At a separate secluded bar* Water can be
piped in for mixing drinks and washing glasses;
or it can be brought in, in a pitcher, and the
glasses taken back to the main sink.
- □ *At a separate bar in a public place* Has the
advantage of being close to the activities it
serves, indoors or out.

Where do you wash your clothes?

- □ *At a commercial laundry*
- □ *At home* This is done in a washer, about
30" wide x 30" deep x 36" high, loaded from
top or front. The washer is generally accompanied by a dryer of about the same size.
Smaller versions of each, about 24" x 24" x 36",
can be bought, and these can be stacked. A
tub is favored by some.

If you wash your clothes at home, where?

- □ *Near where clothes and linen collect and
where people sleep and dress*
- □ *Near where the person who runs the machines
would like to be*
- □ *Isolated in the basement* Inconvenient, but
favored by those who live in terror of the
machines flooding.

Where will people wash their faces and hands?

- □ *In the kitchen sink* Not very glamorous and
provides little privacy, but it's there anyway.
- □ *In a sink near public spaces* Extra expense,
but useful, especially for guests.
- □ *In a sink in a private space* It is almost essential to have a place for washing and groom-
ing near sleeping areas.
- □ *In an isolated sink near a private space*
Provides visual and acoustical privacy, if you
want it, and the advantages of the sink in a
private space.

What kind of sink do you want?

- □ *Mounted on the wall*
- □ *Mounted in a counter*

What size sink do you want?

- [ ] *Standard height*
- [ ] *Higher*
- [ ] *Lower*   Sinks are generally 32″ or 33″ high, which can seem uncomfortably low if you are above medium height. Counters are generally 18″ to 24″ deep.

What color sink do you want?

- [ ] *White*
- [ ] *Other*   The variety of sinks is wide and can be seen at a plumbing showroom.

What kind of accessories do you want near the sink?

- [ ] *Mirrors over it*
- [ ] *Mirrors with lights*   Almost essential; the lights should be either above the mirror or on both sides, not just one side, of the mirror.
- [ ] *A full-length mirror nearby*
- [ ] *Small, movable mirrors*   Helpful to see the side and back of your head.
- [ ] *Shelves or cabinets*   Useful for ointments, medicines, toothpaste, and shaving cream.
- [ ] *Holders for soap*
- [ ] *Holders for toothbrushes*
- [ ] *Holders for razors*
- [ ] *Holders for towels*
- [ ] *Holders for facial tissue*
- [ ] *Convenience outlets for razors, toothbrushes, and the like*
- [ ] *Storage for towels*
- [ ] *Storage for household cleaners*

Do you want many sinks or few? How many can you afford?

- [ ] *One or more near various public areas for individual use*
- [ ] *One near each sleeping area*
- [ ] *One or more shared near sleeping areas*

Where will people wash their whole bodies?

- [ ] *Near sleeping or dressing areas*
- [ ] *Near more-public areas*   As situated, for example, in Charles Moore's house in Orinda.

- [ ] *Somewhere else*   For example, an outdoor shower, if you have a pool or pond or are near the ocean.

What will people wash their bodies in?

- [ ] *Bathtub*   This is the most common device, a receptacle usually 5′ long—though 4′6″, 5′6″, and 6′0″ lengths are also available—by about 2′8″ wide, and about 15″ high. These stand on the floor, or they can, for rather more money, be sunk into it. They are meant to be sat in, though modern ones are not deep enough to contain enough water to cover the recumbent bather. Therefore they are generally combined unsatisfactorily with a spray head built into the wall above.
- [ ] *Bathtub with shower and shower curtain*   Bathtubs thus extended generally are combined with a spray head built into the wall above or fixed at the end of a flexible cable to make a shower. Refinements are available to widen the realm of possible sprays, or to reduce the likelihood of sudden changes in water temperature while you are under it. Some of the spray can be kept in the tub and off the floor by a curtain which will flap around you.
- [ ] *Bathtub with shower and glass doors*   Sliding glass or plastic doors do a better job of keeping the spray in the tub, but they render half of the tub inaccessible.
- [ ] *Fiberglass tubs with shower*   These are obtainable as one-piece units with shower enclosures. They are cheap and easy to install, except in old houses where there may be no doorway large enough to get them through.
- [ ] *Tiled stall shower*   If a stall is large enough (at least 3′ square) it provides a more comfortable shower than one in a tub, though not the possibility of sitting down or soaking. Glass or plastic doors work much better here than on a tub, though curtains are often used for economy. Tile showers look good, are permanent and are easy to clean, except for the joints. They are also relatively expensive.
- [ ] *Plastic laminate stall shower*   Relatively cheap, though corner joints can leak.

□ *Metal stall shower*   Cheap, and looks it. Rusts, except for stainless steel, which looks nice, is not cheap, and can water spot.

□ *One-piece fiberglass stall shower*   Seamless, and so doesn't leak; easy to install in new houses, often difficult in old houses because of its size.

□ *Sauna*   This choice, like the ones which follow below, depends upon the assumption that bathing be an aspect of relaxation. A sauna is a wood-lined room which can be heated to over 200° to induce perspiration which is then meant to be washed off in a cold shower or plunge, though the Finns sometimes roll in the snow.

□ *Steam bath*   Similar to a sauna, but based on steam rather than dry heat.

□ *Japanese bath*   This is a large tub of very hot water for relaxing in after washing.

□ *Swimming pool or plunge, indoors or out*   A more usual alternative to bathing as an aspect of relaxation, it too is generally augmented by a tub or shower, and most often is kept at room temperature or just above. For a plunge, any size larger than a 6'-diameter is acceptable. For serious swimming at least a 40'-length is usually sought. Construction can be of poured or sprayed-on concrete or aluminum or fiberglass, sometimes lined with plastic, above or below the ground.

□ *Relaxation after the bath*   Benches, hammocks, mats, *chaise longues*, deck chairs.

What is your attitude toward privacy in the bath?

□ *Complete privacy*   Offers the security of a small space, and the sense that you cannot be seen.

□ *A bath with a view*   Offers openness to a large indoor space or to the outdoors.

□ *A bath large enough for more than one person*   Affords the company of your family and friends.

What accessories do you need for your bath?

□ *Places for sponges, soap, shampoo, bath oils, brushes*

□ *Places to hang towels and washcloths*
□ *Places to store towels*

Do you want many baths or few?

□ *One near every sleeping and dressing area*
□ *One or more shared between sleeping and dressing areas*
□ *One or more near public areas*

What kind of toilets do you want?

□ *Standing on the floor*   In the United States toilets are designed as basins meant to be sat on at a height of about 14". A space of 30" wide and at least 48" long is required for their use, and to clean around them. Behind the bowl is a tank which holds water, which is released into the bowl after its use, usually with a spinning motion which aids in the washing away of wastes into a continuation of the water system.

□ *Hung from the wall*   More expensive to install, but easier to clean around. It is also more flexible, since it allows the toilet seat to be higher than standard, for ease of rising, or lower, for improved elimination, according to some hygienists. Those who favor lowering it approve of the system used in some countries —notably in Asia—which puts the receptacle even with the floor. Enough Americans are panicked by this idea to restrict the use of such a fixture here.

□ *Special types*   The method of flushing also includes a number of options, from eliminating the tank in favor of a special valve—usually restricted to larger buildings than a house—to various alternatives which reduce odor and noise. Our experience has been that few fancy toilets work so well as the standard, inexpensive ones.

What do you want to combine the toilets with?

□ *Nothing*   Almost always in our society privacy is desired for elimination; if you prefer complete privacy, even from washing and bathing, then your toilet should be kept separate.

245

1. Patio of the Orange Trees, Seville, Spain

☐ *Washing* Can be an economical combination, especially when providing these facilities near public areas.

☐ *Washing and bathing* The standard way, economical of space.

What do you want near the toilets?

☐ *Toilet paper* It should be carefully located, generally low on a nearby wall.

☐ *Reading material* Favored by some.

☐ *Toilet cleansers* Can be conveniently stored near the toilets where they are needed; the storage space can also accommodate extra toilet paper.

What other water sources do you need?

☐ *Drinking fountains*

☐ *Sinks for hobbies* Photography or flower potting, for example.

☐ *Sinks for household cleaning*

☐ *Hose bibbs* For washing cars and windows and watering plants.

What kind of waste disposal facilities will you use?

☐ *Municipal sewers* The waste from each of these fixtures will have to flow away from them—downhill—in pipes standardly 4" in diameter, much larger than the pipes which brought the water. If the municipal sewer can be found only above the house, then sewage must be pumped up to it. The pumps are expensive—several hundred dollars—but available. The municipal authorities will also be concerned about ground or storm water which will have to be led in trenches or channels or gravel-filled trenches—called French drains—or across sloping ground to where it can proceed downhill from your property without endangering neighboring land.

☐ *Septic tanks* These are large, sunken, concrete boxes where bacteria consume the solid waste. The liquid then flows into a system of perforated pipes, or a series of underground chambers from which it leaches into the soil. The appropriate experts or officials must test your soil to determine its capacity to absorb the liquid. Again, if suitable ground for leaching can only be found above the house, then liquid sewage must be pumped up to it.

It is helpful to note that all this delivery and use of water and the disposal of water-born waste forms a continuous system, downhill all the way, except when pumps raise it. If you are of a visual frame of mind, it should be helpful to make a linear diagram which shows the continuousness of this system and pinpoints the places where it intersects the other continuous systems we shall describe, such as the one which brings in food and takes out garbage. As you imagine these continuous systems, you can consider the economic and intellectual advantages of shortening and clarifying them. The Patio of the Orange Trees adjoining the cathedral at Seville presents a famous instance where the path of the water being led to the orange trees forms the basis for the visual order of the design. (1) The internal water distributing system of a house, hidden largely in pipes, is unlikely to produce that much visual drama, but the chance to make it clearer to the mind (as well as cheaper) remains.

Air

Another system of paths, even less visible than the water in its pipes and channels, is made by the air as it drifts through our houses, or is warmed or cooled by machines and then blown through.

The visible evidence of air moving through houses, especially in the heat of the summer, has been a source of pleasure for a long time. Thin curtains blowing at the windows, a fan in the ceiling gently turning, the airborne sound of buzzing bees, the scent of lilacs drifting in the open window—all enrich our enjoyment and deepen our comfort, while, for centuries, the source of warmth radiated from an open fire has been almost synonymous with the concept of "home." By now, the temperature and even the amount of air, cooled or heated, which is delivered to us through ducts or pipes (and for our present purposes we will consider piped water in heating and cooling systems as part of the air paths) is far more precisely controlled, and the rich overtones are gone.

Also included with the paths of air are the filters and stops which control sun and sound and smell and exclude airborne insects. The controls with the longest histories, like screened porches, awnings, shutters, and chimneys, conjure up images of their own, not yet—for most of us—marked by ducts and dampers, though an aesthetic of ducts and conduits does animate some modern architecture, notably that of a British group called Archigram.

How do you want to capture cooling breezes?

☐ *Orienting the openings* The difficulties of capturing an errant breeze are compensated for by the delicious reward of the breeze itself. If you want to capture breezes, you should discover which way they are likely to come from, then make use of the Venturi principle. Orient small openings to windward, so the breezes can build up and rush in. Place larger openings to leeward through which the air can flow, speeded up as it joins breezes blown over the top of the building.

☐ *Other techniques* For hot desert climates especially, there is a whole tradition of ways to lead the dry air past pools or plants, so that evaporation from them will cool the breeze.

What kind of cooling system do you want?

☐ *Central air conditioning* To create eternal spring. Especially in very hot or muggy climates, or in densely populated or dirty or noisy places, this has the approval of almost everyone. Air can be cleaned before it gets in

the house, and unwanted noises and burglars are readily excluded. The temperature is chosen, not chanced on, and air circulation can be closely controlled. These units can be combined with the furnace and share its ducts or pipes. In central air-conditioning systems there is a condenser, generally about 3′ in diameter, with a fan blowing up, which must be put outside or on the roof. It is connected through pipes preferably under 50′ long with the chiller unit. The pipes, or especially the ducts, describe another path through the house. Again, economy, with its conceptual as well as monetary justifications, occurs when the pattern is clear and spare.

☐ *Room air conditioners* These fit into windows or, if you prefer not to lose the light and view, into a wall. They are relatively inexpensive.

☐ *Windows* Old-fashioned; often very pleasant; inexpensive.

☐ *Some of each* An option is to count on the breezes until they give out, then turn on the air conditioning as a last resort, so you prepare yourself either way.

If you want to capture the winter sun, how?

☐ *South-facing and partially enclosed spaces outdoors* In most climates, the fickle winter sun is the cold-weather counterpart of summer's breezes. The warmth of it on your face in a sheltered space outdoors is delicious and the chance to sit in it to read or nap is much to be prized.

☐ *South-facing windows* The warming rays of the sun come through glass—though its ultraviolet rays which provide a suntan come only through special glass—and are undeterred by the insulating glass which helps keep the warm air inside. Its presence can markedly reduce winter fuel bills and add to the pleasures of winter habitation. Note, however, that in the summertime, south-facing windows will admit more sun and therefore more heat than you probably want. There are several ways to cope with this problem. One, obviously, is to install movable awnings. Another depends upon the fact that in the winter the sun is low in the sky and in summer it is high; so permanent sunscreens or eaves can be placed above windows in a way that allows the sun to enter during the winter months, but to be blocked in the summer. Still another way—perhaps the most natural and pleasant of all—is to plant deciduous trees outside south-facing windows.

What kind of heating system do you want?

☐ *Radiant* Radiation sends heat from a warmer surface to a cooler one—you. It is independent of the intervening air temperature, even as the sun warms us through the absolute cold of outer space, or as a fireplace warms us in a cold room.
☐ *Convecting* Convection warms the air around you, either by its being blown at you from the place it was warmed up, or by passing over warmed pipes. In spite of its name, a radiator works by convection.

What kind of circulation system do you want for the heat?

☐ *Hot air* Heated air is sent through ducts to registers in each room and returned to the furnace through one or more additional registers.
☐ *Hot water* This is sent in pipes along baseboards, or in radiant surfaces like floors and ceilings.
☐ *Electric* This uses resistance wires to heat up wall or ceiling panels.

What kind of fuel will you use?

☐ *Gas*
☐ *Oil*
☐ *Electricity*
☐ *Other* These days the decision about fuel has strong ecological overtones, but there is no clear winner. The cheapest fuel, in most areas, is oil or gas. Oil must be stored in tanks; gas is not always available. Gas produces little pollution; finer oils pollute less than heavier ones—which often contain sulphur—but cost more. Electricity is expensive, though its initial costs are slightly less; it is clean at your house,

but open to the charge that its manufacturer is polluting air or water somewhere. You can hear the arguments from your local utilities and weigh them against costs in your area.

Do you want a constant temperature everywhere, or variations?

☐ *Constant temperature* The advent of central heating and air conditioning has made it possible to have 70° everywhere at all times, with all the comfort—and monotony— that that implies.
☐ *Desirable variations* The advent of central heating has not destroyed the possibility of varying temperatures from room to room. One of the devices for mapping dwellings has been the patterns of heat and cold, especially in the winter. Fireplaces have been focal points; even the tapestries on palatial stone walls have been there as much to provide a warmer surface and a softer one, for sound control, as for their decorative effect. Some places have been made comfortable to sit on cold nights, others only comfortable to walk through. Japanese housebuilders, on islands with extremes of temperature, have framed their architecture with a mind to the soggy summer, and they handle the winters altogether sketchily; the occupants huddle under quilts and light charcoal braziers, the better to pursue some aesthetic goals. In our houses the sun in our faces feels much better when we're a little chilly. But note that there can be variations in temperature which you don't want, like chilly air blowing down from a cold window to where you want to sit, or hot air in summer rising to unventilated high pockets where perhaps you want to be.

What filters the air?

☐ *Windows*
☐ *Screens*
☐ *Bars*
☐ *Mosquito nets*
☐ *Other filters* Filtering can happen at any scale, through openings large enough to admit people, but not horses, or small enough to admit air, but not pollen. Windows augmented

by grills can be arranged to admit breezes while they exclude intruders; provided with screens, they can exclude flying insects while they admit air. Mosquito nets around sleeping places, for instance, can provide another line of defense against the insects which bypass the first filter. Sophisticated three-dimensional filters can be installed as part of your ventilation system, even using electrostatic pressure to trap pollution or dirt or moisture. Every exclusion, of course, impedes the desirable flow of air and to some extent the amount of air movement you seek.

What kind of windows do you want?

☐ *Glass or plastic* Glass is by far the most usual choice, but transparent or translucent plastic is sometimes used where glass would be particularly likely to break.

☐ *Single or double glazing* Double glazing is often used in rigorous climates, with a sealed space between the two sheets to inhibit condensation and improve insulation.

☐ *Wood or metal frames* Steel is strong, but must be painted, and the paint often flakes off. Aluminum can be anodized to a dark gray or bronze color. Metal frames in cold climates can allow moisture to condense. Wood cannot.

How do you want the windows to admit air?

☐ *Sliding horizontally* This is generally the most economical, since the frame doesn't have to be so strong, and indeed the 6'8" high by 8' wide sliding glass door with an aluminum frame usually provides the largest window for the least money. Smaller sliding windows are similarly economical.

☐ *Sliding vertically* Double-hung windows, which slide vertically, are almost as economical as windows that slide horizontally. They generally come with spring-loaded reels for keeping the sash at the desired height.

☐ *Swinging from the side* As casements, which can swing out to catch air coming from an angle.

☐ *Swinging from the top* As awnings. Both types of swinging windows require sturdy frames, in case they are caught by a sudden gust of wind.

☐ *Vertical pivoting windows*

☐ *Horizontal pivoting windows* Both types balance more easily than swinging windows, but they pose almost insoluble problems of insect screening.

☐ *Fixed glass* Some architects have made a point of separating the glass—for seeing through—from the opening for air, which comes then through separate louvers. This aids in excluding rainstorms and burglars and allows you to look out through glass unmarred by insect screening. But it inserts a curious denial, making it impossible to open up directly to the outdoors and its breath of air.

☐ *Storm windows* A casualty of the development of sealed double glass panes has been storm windows, which in some places used to replace insect screening for the winter months. Though their installation was an annual pain, the ceremonial marking of the passage of the seasons, the change which came with the added brightness when the screens were removed, and—sometimes—the extra pattern of another set of mullions provided another device for enlivening the act of habitation. Indeed, in some instances, the space between the inner and the outer glass is carefully formed and takes on a life of its own, as in a window greenhouse or Alvar Aalto's Vuoksenniska Church in Imatra, Finland. (2)

How do you want to filter the sound that goes with the air?

☐ *Compromise* Most of the sounds that surround us and drive us wild are airborne, though some are telegraphed through structures, or drummed through solid walls. The best way to keep a wall from allowing sound to pass is to make it heavy. The best way to block airborne noise is to block the air. Even a keyhole or the crack around a door lets some sound through. Since stopping the sound is in conflict with many of the demands for comfort based on the passage of warm or cool air, the conflict has to be resolved by careful compro-

2. Vuoksenniska Church, Imatra, Finland, by Alvar Aalto, 1957

mise. Remember that sounds are made not only by loved ones, but as well by cars, trucks, and airplanes outside. The acousticians' concept of "white sound" or "acoustical perfume" is worth noting here: you might well want to drown out unwanted sounds with, say, a fountain or a fan, rather than trying against all odds to exclude them.

Paper

For most of us, the path of paper coming into and out of our houses is at flood tide. Mountains of mail (important and junk), magazines, daily newspapers, wrappings, boxes, cartons, all conspire to swamp us. The fight to identify survivors in the flood (licenses, letters, lists) occasions an almost daily crisis in most houses. You must plan to keep this flood within its banks, to establish a path along which paper will travel, rescue points, storage arrangements, and an easy way out for the waste. The reservoirs for storage have to be large enough to let the paper pile up during periods when there is no time to sort it. The following places should be seen as points on a path. Again, economy suggests a simple and clear passage.

How does the paper come in?

- ☐ *Newspapers delivered*
- ☐ *Mail delivered*
- ☐ *Carried in by you*

What do you do with it, and where?

- ☐ *Sort it*
- ☐ *Read it*
- ☐ *File it*
- ☐ *Write on more paper in response to the message on the incoming paper*
- ☐ *Display it*
- ☐ *Throw it away*   The sorting and reading areas may be of special importance to some people, who should consider these places for comfort, adequacy, and even view. The display

of anything important, like the children's drawings, gives added point to the whole process. The throwing away may have to be dramatized with a giant mouth or a chrome waste can to speed the paper's departure.

For the paper that goes away, how does it go?

- ☐ *Mailing*
- ☐ *Recycling*
- ☐ *Disposing*   A trash bin is essential, and a fireplace or incinerator can be helpful.

Who takes it away? From where? To where?

- ☐ *You*
- ☐ *Municipal garbage service*
- ☐ *Private garbage service*   In our country the surest sign of housing for poor people, or of poor housing for middle-income people, is the uncontrolled accumulation of paper and trash. Figuring out what to do with yours to avoid frustration from children, dogs, raccoons, and the sheer hopelessness of trying to cram too much stuff into too little space deserves high priority in planning your house.

Food

The tides of foodstuffs into our houses and out again are generally under considerably closer control than the tides of papers. For one thing, we pay for the food, so we are careful. But the food bulks large, and sacks of it are heavy. So a clear path affects economies of effort here, too.

Where does the food come from?

- ☐ *Carried by you from up the street to where it will be stored.*
- ☐ *Carried by you from your car to where it will be stored.*
- ☐ *Delivered by someone who may arrive when you are not at home.*

Where in the house does it go?

- ☐ *Somewhere to be sorted*   Foods which need refrigeration can then be given it quickly, and other foods can go where they belong. The need for economy on this path will manifest itself to you every time you come home from the supermarket. For most of us it is the trip from the automobile to the kitchen counter which should be most carefully mapped.

Where will it be stored?

☐ *A refrigerator* Provides space for short-term cold storage, and some for long-term storage in the freezer compartment. Refrigerators can stand upright, or they can be bought to fit under a 36"-high counter. They are usually 25" deep, and their widths vary with their capacity, from about 24" up.

☐ *A freezer* Freezers have traditionally come as chests opened from the top, but that type is giving way to freezers shaped like a refrigerator, with doors on the front. These lose their cold air more quickly when you open them, but are more economical of space. They come, too, with a variety of devices for making, storing, and even tumbling out ice cubes.

☐ *Shelves* The standard kitchen format restricts these food storage areas to the space under the counter (2'-deep shelves which must be burrowed into from a kneeling or crouching position) and, better, the shelves above the counter, usually at about 55" and 67", with one at 79" available to tall people. These are standardly shallower than the shelves below the counter, about 15" deep, so they are more convenient, but there are usually too few of them.

☐ *Bins* Useful for storing loose foods, such as potatoes or onions.

☐ *Canisters* Useful for storing sugar, flour, coffee, and the like.

☐ *Spice racks*

☐ *Pantry storage* Shelves not deeper than 12" can go from floor to head height or above, so that the items stored will be visible. This type of storage provides a useful and accommodating arrangement for boxes and sacks and cans of food. The shelves can be fronted with cabinet doors; or for less money, with ordinary doors to the floor; or even less expensively,

they can be left open, to give householders so inclined the chance to arrange the containers as a changing display of color and shapes.

☐ *Liquor and wine storage* Special provision must be made for bottles of liquor, and especially of wine, which should be on its side in a cool place. Here, perhaps, a little distance strengthens the ritual of choosing a bottle.

Where will food be opened and prepared?

☐ *A counter* Food has to be taken out of the refrigerator or freezer or off the shelf, put somewhere while you collect your thoughts, then opened, or washed, or whatever it requires. This probably will happen on a counter near the sink and, preferably, near the refrigerator, too. This counter is the place for any machines meant to change the shape of food by beating, chopping, mixing, pureeing, or liquefying it. And it is the place as well to discard the packages in which the food has come. Standard height is 36" above the floor, higher if you are tall, lower if you are short. If you want to sit down for this part of the food preparation, you can have a surface at desk height—28" or 29"—with a place for your knees beneath. Alternatively, of course, you can have a high stool.

How will food be heated up?

☐ *Gas*
☐ *Electricity*

What kind of burners do you prefer?

☐ *Ones combined with one or two ovens to make a standard stove*
☐ *Ones mounted in the counter*

What kind of oven or ovens do you prefer?

☐ *One or two in a standard stove*
☐ *One or two mounted under or above the counter* The advantage of separate ovens lies in the chance to put them high enough so they can be looked into and their contents removed

or put in without stooping. Ovens under burners are harder to stoop down for, but they save space, and generally cost less. Some one-piece stoves come with an eye-level oven above and another oven below.

What other cooking devices do you want?

- ☐ *Toaster*
- ☐ *Coffee pot*
- ☐ *Electric frying pan*
- ☐ *Fondue pot*
- ☐ *Other*   There is a vast assortment of cooking devices for specific purposes, and these can be located with considerable flexibility, though almost all of them require electricity. They can even be at the place where the food will be eaten.

Where is the food eaten?

- ☐ *Where it is prepared*   When speed or effortlessness dictates, this can be done by people standing or sitting or perched on high stools.
- ☐ *A special place for eating*   This should be close to where the food is warmed; if this place is used for breakfast and lunch, most people would prefer it to be in the sun, hopefully with a pleasant outlook. More extended dining, on the other hand, falls into the realm of onstage ritual or improvisation in a room. Ritual here carries images of a table big enough for everyone, with at least 2′ of perimeter per person to be served, enough space to get there and maneuver a chair, as well as a place for serving. The conditions of this space can be carefully set: is the view—if you want one —visible after sunset? Can the lights be controlled? Improvisation also suggests the chance to eat where the mood allows, outdoors, or by the television, or in the greenhouse, or in bed; it requires encouragement or suggestion: tables outdoors, for instance, can increase the likelihood of people's eating there.

What is the fate of what remains?

- ☐ *Restorage of usable leftovers*

- ☐ *Removal of unusable leftovers by a garbage disposer in the sink*   Only certain remains can be gotten rid of here.
- ☐ *Trash cans for the rest of the unusable leftovers*
- ☐ *Trash compactors for the rest of the unusable leftovers*   Here again our path intersects with the monumental trash problem. We have excess food, and the armatures it comes on (bones and corn cobs and the like) and the often wet and gooey paper and plastic and metal it came in. The food in many houses is ground up in a disposal mechanism in the sink and washed away, but the armatures and packings stay as trash. Trash compressors, still rare and expensive, are now on the market to squeeze down this problem. But usually an easy, convenient, and sanitary path, with storage reservoirs enroute, must be found to get the garbage, with a minimum of odor and mess, away from the cooking area and out of the house, to a place where it can safely be given to someone else—a garbage collector, not dogs or rats or children.

Dishes and other cooking utensils
A path closely related to that of the food is that of the vessels it is prepared in or served on. These vessels, as well as glasses, flatware, and utensils of silver, pewter, copper, and glass are, for some, of great importance, made with great care, and cherished. Others prefer to eat from paper plates. Dishes arrive in the house infrequently enough to let us assume that they are already there. But there is nevertheless their storage to consider.

Where will you store dishes, flatware, cooking utensils, vases, and ashtrays?

- ☐ *On shelves where they can be seen by visitors and by you*   These might be in the main rooms of your house or in the area where the food is going to be put on them. They might be on open shelves or behind glass.
- ☐ *In cabinets where they are not on display*   The main concern, then, is for convenience to

the point where they will be used and to the point where they will be washed.

- □ *Hanging from pegs or racks* This is favored by some for pots and pans.
- □ *Divided among the locations where they will be used* This division should occur if there is a separate bar or service kitchen or dishwashing area, or if you are anxious to separate vessels destined for special occasions from those you use everyday.
- □ *In, or out of, reach of children* So they can help; or so dishes can be safe from them.

Where will you use the dishes?

- □ *On a counter or table near the sink* For preparing food and serving it.
- □ *On buffets, tables, counters or laps*
- □ *At bars, at the bedside, at coffee tables*

Where will you wash the dishes?

- □ *At sinks or dishwashers* Here the dishes cross the path of the water.

Then how will you conveniently store the dishes again?

- □ *Proximate* You should be able to replace them on their shelves or hooks without a walk with each dish.
- □ *Collected for storage* If you want to store dishes far from where they are going to be washed, a tea tray, a dumbwaiter, or even a simple tray might be used. If it is a tray, there must be a place to put it—loaded—at each end of its trip. If it is a tea tray, with wheels, there must be maneuvering room for it and storage space.

Clothing and linen

Next to food and water, perhaps the most familiar elements of domesticity are the pieces of cloth which we use to clothe us, or to surround us, in bed or out, or to dry our bodies or other objects. Though pieces of cloth qualify sometimes as light control at windows, sometimes as purely decorative objects, and even occasionally as art, a characteristic of most of the cloth in our houses is that it is generally collected, washed and dried, put away, and used again, and so it describes a chartable path through the house.

What happens to clothing when it first enters the house?

- □ *It's taken off* A place to put outer garments when you enter is required in most climates. In cold climates, the garments can be very bulky and require extensive space on hooks or in a closet. The coats may be dripping with rain or snow and require provision for the water to drain off, and they may be accompanied by hats and umbrellas, also soaking wet. In some climates the snow or rain you bring in may be mixed with mud, especially on your outer footwear, suggesting the provision of a special "mud room" with a waterproof floor and a place to sit down and remove the offending garments.
- □ *It is stored temporarily* If you patronize a commercial laundry, then packages of clean clothes and garments on hangers may be one of the most frequent deliveries at your house. If you want provision for deliveries to be made when you are not at home, you should plan for that.

Where does the clothing go for longer-term storage?

- □ *Into closets* Some clothes hang on hangers, others more easily lie on shelves or in drawers. To be really precise about sizes you should measure your own garments, folded or hung as you like them. The rule of thumb is that closets accommodating garments on hangers must be at least 2' deep. The standard provision is for a pole about 5'6" above the floor, which should accommodate your longest garments, though it leaves considerable wasted space below shorter ones, like jackets or shirts, and some wasted space above as well. One simple economy is to put a rod as high as you can comfortably reach, then put a rod for part of its length below it, so that shorter garments can be doubled up. You should also consider alternative ways of hanging up clothes—slits, rods, or clips for storing trousers, skirts, and other pieces of clothing which do not have to be on hangers. Many articles of clothing can be folded and kept in drawers or, even more simply, on shelves. These drawers or shelves do not normally need to be more than 18″ deep, so space is lost if they are mixed with the hanging space, but still other items, such as shoes, hats, purses, and umbrellas, might be fitted into the still empty space above and below the hanging clothes. The issue of closure for the closets also stirs debate. One recourse is to leave them open. Another is regular swinging doors, but these require space in the adjoining room. Sliding doors hide half the closet at any one time. Bi-fold doors are convenient and fairly inexpensive, but to some they look it. Curtains flap into the way. The old-fashioned walk-in closet, entered through a single door, provides a surprisingly effective combination of enclosure and ease of access to the contents. But it takes more space than any other alternative. Your decisions should include what kind of closet you need and how big; you can best judge by measuring what you have and adding a factor for growth.

☐ *Wardrobes*
☐ *Chests of drawers*

Where should the closets be?

☐ *In or near sleeping areas*
☐ *In or near bathing areas*   This is a question of your habits—whether, for instance, you bathe just before you dress—and of your preferences—whether, for instance, you would like to have your sleeping area free of clothes or separate so where you sleep can be cold and where you dress can be warm.

Where does the soiled clothing go?

☐ *Out of the house to a commercial laundry*
   In this case you'll want convenient stations for collecting it and perhaps a chute or cart to take it to a central place.
☐ *To be washed on the premises*   The washing can be near the places where the dirty clothes collect or at the end of a chute from those places.

How is it dried?

☐ *In a dryer*   They come gas or electric.
☐ *By hanging indoors*   Permanent-press garments, especially, need to drip-dry from hangers. There needs to be a place for the hangers and something underneath which will not be damaged by water dripping onto it.
☐ *By hanging outdoors*   A nuisance, but there is not yet a replacement for the sweet smell of cloth which has dried in the sun and breeze.

How does it get ironed?

☐ *On an ironing board*   It can be built in or portable, in the kitchen or laundry room or just about anywhere else you want.
☐ *By being hand-blocked*   As sweaters should be.
☐ *Not at all*   By being permanent-press fabric.

How do you prefer to get it back?

☐ *With least effort, by washing and drying it nearby*
☐ *In a cart or dumbwaiter*   Laundry is heavy and carrying it can be difficult.

   Another great part of household cloth is bed linen, sheets, and pillow cases of smooth fabric. The current sleeping practice in the United States, as in much of the rest of the world, requires soft horizontal surfaces, mattresses, generally made with foam rubber or plastic, or of coiled metal springs padded with cotton, supported a few inches above the floor on a hard slab or on metal springs, flat or coiled. Mattresses come in standard sizes. Mattress pads are available, to keep the mattress clean, for every size. So are sheets, either flat and big enough to tuck in around or "contour," so that they fit neatly over either two or four corners of the mattress. On top of two sheets are piled blankets or quilts or comforters, sometimes electrically warmed, though the trend to unchanging room temperatures may hasten the retirement of some of these. Pillows of feathers or of foam rubber or of Dacron are generally added, covered with sheeting fashioned into a pillowcase. Great care used to be lavished on the embellishment of sheets and pillowcases with tatting, crochet, or embroidery. That embellishment is infrequent now, but a wide variety of available colors and patterns has replaced it.

The main problem today is that the rather elaborate layering of bedclothes, and the attendant assumption that not making the bed is in some way reprehensible, leaves us with a daily chore less and less appropriate to the mood of machine-aided carefree living prized by almost all of us. Perhaps handsome washable sleeping bags will free us from the daily chore, as well as the attachment to all those specific mattress sizes.

What size beds do you want? How many of each?

☐ *Cot 30" x 74"*
☐ *Single bed 36" x 74"*
☐ *Twin bed 39" x 74"*
☐ *Three-quarter bed 48" x 74"*
☐ *Double bed 54" x 74"*
Each of the above is available long, usually 76"; also available are:
☐ *Queen size 60" x 76"*
☐ *King size 78" x 76"*

Where will you store your bed linen?

☐ *In the bedroom closet*
☐ *In a linen closet*
☐ *In the laundry room*
☐ *Elsewhere*

How will you get your bed linen to where it will be washed?

☐ *Carry it*
☐ *Put it down a chute*
☐ *Cart it*

How will you return it to its storage place?

☐ *Carry it*
☐ *Send it up in a dumbwaiter*
☐ *Cart it*

Elaborate table linen has accompanied elaborate bed linen into limbo. Not very long ago tablecloths and napkins, like sheets and pillowcases, provided the excuse for the lavishing of prenuptial care. Now, not only the embroidery has departed, but the tablecloths often have, too, replaced by paper place mats and even napkins. To the extent that either of these have become paper, they follow the route of the paper flood tide. Those which remain cloth describe a tributary to the flow of other cloth through the house.

Where will you store the table linen?

☐ *In the cooking area*
☐ *Near the eating area*

How will you take it to the area where it can be washed?

☐ *Carry it*
☐ *Put it down a chute*
☐ *Cart it*

How will you wash and iron it?

☐ *Send to commercial laundry*
☐ *Wash and dry and iron it at home*
☐ *Stick to permanent press*

How will you bring it back to where it is stored?

☐ *Carry it, since there is little enough*
☐ *Put it in a dumbwaiter*
☐ *Cart it*

Another branch of the cloth flow still very much with us is the provision of towels for the sinks and the baths. These run the gamut from the fingertip towels (which are meant to look destroyed after one using and which unaccountably persist in powder rooms) to the enveloping terry towels (bath sheets) and robes which add pleasure to drying off after bathing. What they all have in common is their need, after one or a few uses, to be washed and dried.

Where are they stored?

☐ *At the bathing areas*
☐ *Where they are washed*
☐ *Elsewhere*

Where are they used?

☐ *At sinks*
☐ *At bathing areas*   Since they are often used repeatedly, they must be hung on racks so they may dry out between wettings. Pipes make useful racks; some are even heated, by running hot water through them, to hasten the drying of towels on them and to make the towels themselves more pleasant to the touch.

How do they get to point of washing?

☐ *Carried*
☐ *Carted*
☐ *Chuted*
☐ *Dumbwaitered*

Similarly, you should trace the path of kitchen towels and any other pieces of regularly washable cloth you plan on having in your house. Once more, making the path clearer has its own special virtues at least equal to the day-by-day practical advantages

you gain from not having dirty laundry lying all around. But remember, the laundry for the average household still weighs a great deal, and you should not condemn yourself, by a lack of planning, to a lifetime of lugging it.

Electricity

No charting of paths would be complete without following the route of the electricity whose passage animates your house. Its influence is felt well beyond its own path, since electricity broadcasts itself in artificial light, heat, recorded sound, and a host of other ways. Unlike water, it doesn't show up unannounced: you have to make a deal with your utility company, or manufacture it yourself.

In the United States two strengths of electricity are generally available: 110 volts, for most household uses, and 220 volts, for such heavy appliances as electric stoves and some air-conditioning systems. In the case of the 110 volts, the voltage comes in two wires, and the appliance connected to them completes the circuit and turns on. The 220 volts come normally with three wires, and again the appliance completes the circuit. In an analogy with water, the volts are electrical *pressure*. Amps, or amperes, are the *amount* of electricity, and watts, which are volts multiplied by amps, represent the total flow. Each appliance carries a rating in watts, and you are billed for the number of watts, or kilowatts (1000 watts) you use in a month. The electricity coursing through your house is broken, for convenience and safety, into separate circuits, normally of about 15 amps each, each of which allows 110 volts times 15 amps, or 1650 watts. If you plug in appliances with more watts than that, you overload the circuit, and a circuit breaker snaps off the current to avert catastrophe. Some circuits are heavier, to accommodate the appliances which need more electricity (220 volts, for instance, times 20 amps is 4400 watts, more than enough for an electric stove).

Electric wire is quite cheap and nowadays is generally concealed, so it can be argued that its mere presence is more important than the formal clarity of its path. The same is true for other wiring systems, telephone and television, for instance. Nevertheless, the opportunity remains, if you want it, to make the paths the wires trace through your house a visual and conceptual statement. The old-fashioned knob-and-tube system, in which insulated wires ran exposed, held away from wood surfaces and from each other by white porcelain fittings, has been outlawed by most codes, and wiring is required in most places to be run in a flexible conduit of metal or plastic or in rigid metal pipes, so it is the conduit, fixtures, and junction boxes, not the wire inside, whose path you will make visible.

Many electric light fixtures are in about the state of visual development reached by the automobile in 1902, when the imitation of the horse-drawn carriage was still ardently attempted. Present-day light fixtures often try to imitate candles (in which case the bright point sources can give pain to the eyes), or they imitate lanterns or hurricane lamps (in which case the light source, presumably located so the wind won't blow it out, can be so deeply concealed that it affords little illumination). The best hope seems to lie in light sources large and dim enough to avoid hurting the eyes, and in indirect or shielded sources bright and efficient enough to perform their tasks. Interestingly, the simple table lamp with a translucent shade performs both of the functions admirably.

The possibilities in the design of fixtures and, especially, of the light they cast are almost unlimited. As we've noted, modern design has not yet bestowed on light those subtleties attendant on change of brightness and quality and direction which natural light affords. But artificial light does have the power to create a mood (albeit a relatively unchanging one), to bring focus to a space or suggest motion through it. The present technician-led tendency is to demand a level of light that is high and uniform, like the 70° temperature of the house, except that the illuminating industry seems annually to raise the required brightness level.

Where is the electricity to come from?

☐ *A public power source*   Almost certainly.
☐ *Your own generator*   If you live in the boondocks.

How will it arrive?

☐ *On overhead wires*   These are usually regarded, justifiably, as environmental blight. But if there aren't too many, and if the landscape allows, they can have an expressive function attesting the entry of power, an electric attachment, to the rest of the world. An early scheme of ours introduced a pylon to receive the wires from overhead electricity and telephone systems. If the wiring in the street is overhead, you face a choice whether to have it enter the house overhead from the pole, or to go underground from the pole to the house. The latter, of course, costs more, but bypasses visual blight.
☐ *Underground*   If the public supply is underground, then of course your house can be supplied underground too, for electric and telephone wires.

Where does it arrive?

☐ *At a meter box*   It must be available to the person who reads the meter.
☐ *Then at the main panel board*   It must

be readily accessible to you when an overload trips the circuit breakers.

Where does the system go?

☐ *To light sources* Describe the places where you want light.
☐ *To convenience outlets* The code will usually demand that you have a double convenience outlet centered on every 12' of wall. Remember to provide not only for lamps and fixed appliances, but for movable ones, such as a vacuum cleaner, as well.
☐ *To switches* Include three-way and four-way switches when you want the capacity to turn lights off from a place different from where you turned them on. Insist that switches be conveniently located and easy to find. You can, if you'd like, install a bank of switches, perhaps by your bed, to turn on lights all over the house to detect or scare prowlers. You may also be interested in low-voltage systems, either for switches or for auxiliary lighting outside. A low-voltage system requires transformers, but then operates on voltage pressure low enough to allow, for instance, direct burial of wires without danger of short circuits or fire.
☐ *To dimmers* The most obvious chance for varying artificial light over a period of time.
☐ *To doorbells and thermostats* These use low-voltage wires.

What other systems of wires are there?

☐ *Telephone* With wires to all the places where a telephone might be desired or its long cord might be plugged in.
☐ *TV and FM antennas or cable television*
☐ *Sound systems* For music in whatever rooms you desire it. Don't forget storage of tapes and/or records.
☐ *Lightning rods*

Dirt

A path maker as compulsory as water, but far less desired, is dirt. It blows in or is tracked into your house, then periodically has to be removed. Virtue consists in preventing accumulation and facilitating removal.

How may dirt be kept out in the first place?

☐ *By filtering outside air* Instead of letting it blow in naturally.
☐ *By providing mats, vestibules or mud rooms* To intercept dirt being tracked in.

How may it be controlled?

☐ *By providing smooth surfaces*
☐ *By minimizing objects to be dusted* You may well deduce that having soft surfaces or objects you enjoy around you is more important than minimum dusting.

How may it be removed?

☐ *With dust cloths or dusters*
☐ *With mops*
☐ *With brooms*
☐ *With carpet sweeper*
☐ *With vacuum cleaner* Where will it be? Together with its accessory parts and a dustpan it should be stored near to the places where it will be used. Or the vacuum cleaner can be expanded, at some cost, into a system built into the walls which pulls the vacuumed dirt to a central place.

Where will the dirt be taken?

☐ *Washed down a sink* From a wet mop. Do you want a special sink?
☐ *Removed with the trash* If trash receptacles can take sweepings.
☐ *Specially taken to the disposal area* When vacuum cleaner bag is emptied, or a filter removed.

Again, paths planned in advance will save hours later.

Automobiles

By far the widest path on your premises (after the bulldozers have come and gone) will be made by your car, or cars. They are much less flexible in their maneuvering than are people on foot: they do not readily go upstairs or make right-angle turns; and they are big. The main question about their presence is your attitude toward them: do you love your cars and want them near you? Or do you hate them and seek to mask their presence? The unacknowledged ambivalence has confused and deadened many an American suburban house.

How will the cars arrive at your house?

- □ *Never* If you really hate them, you can stop them somewhere short of the house and walk in.
- □ *On a driveway* It must be straight enough to move a car along it, and not too steep: 10% slope should be maximum, though where there is no snow 15% is accepted by the brave. The driveway can be narrow, no more than 10' wide if you will not meet cars head-on or have to back out of it. A circle with a diameter of 60' is needed to avoid backing and filling.

Where will they arrive at your house?

- □ *At an entrance courtyard* Which might be partly surrounded by the house and will give onto main and service entrances.
- □ *At a garage* What will visitors do if they can't fit in the garage?
- □ *At a service entrance* How will visitors get to where you want them?

Where will you store your car or cars?

- □ *Outside* Cars are built to stand it, but deep snow fallen on them may be a nuisance.
- □ *Outside under cover* Now only drifting snow can trap them, and they can be entered under cover during a rain storm.

- □ *In a garage* Here they can be dry, and even warm, if you want to pay for that. A space at least 12' x 22' should be provided for each car, so a double garage could be the largest room in your house. Does that fit your priorities? Or might it, if you used the garage sometimes for other uses? Remember that the car is about as continent as a large puppy, and grease drips from its underside.

How will you get from car to your house?

- □ *Through a service entrance*
- □ *Through a main entrance*
- □ *Along a passage* This can put the cars at arm's length, without sending you into the rain.

Other objects

The possibilities for other objects to chart a path to or through your house are just about endless. We note five classes of objects which may deserve your special consideration: we shall ask whether you have them, then leave it to you to chart their paths.

Some objects are sufficiently large to merit special attention: skis, a lawn mower, bicycles, a grand piano, a set of drums, all move their ways rather bulkily into the house, requiring thought about their paths in and out and to the place they are kept. What large items must you accommodate? What paths do they take? Where will they be kept?

Some other objects require special attention because they are treasured, and extra care must be exercised to prevent their being marred or broken or mislaid or stolen. Collections might lie in this category. What treasures will you accommodate? What paths will they take? Where will they be kept? How will they be secured?

Some objects deserve special attention because they are of special interest to you, or you have a large number of them, even if they're not terribly fragile or valuable. If you have a collection of books, for example, you may want to keep them in a special order. What objects of special interest will you accommodate? What paths will they take? Where will they be kept?

Other objects may get special attention because their unattractive qualities earn them a wide berth. Gym clothes after they have been worn are eligible, or perhaps your child collects snakes. What objects in your house need isolation? What paths will they take? Where will they be confined?

A fifth class of objects requires the concealment which dirty books used to get, and may again. A bottle of blond hair rinse, for instance, or a sack of marijuana may require a special place safe from the children or the cleaning lady or your nosier friends. What objects in your house need concealment? Along what paths will you hustle them into concealment? How will you furtively retrieve them?

Adults

So far we have described only the paths of *things*, and if we have been complete, have mapped along these paths the machines and machine realms of your house. What has only been hinted at so far are the rooms, the empty stages which now require your interpretation of what your actions will be, and how you intend to occupy the stages. What you need is to note carefully your preferences for the kinds of places you want to be in. Doing this will bring up such issues as: whether you will move widely (*sweep* down the stairs), tightly (*squeeze* into a niche), or not at all (be in repose); whether you will be formally dressed, informally dressed, or undressed; therefore whether you will be in the mood for display or seeking shelter from view;

alone, with another, or in a group; indoors or out, or at the edge; in a large or a small space; served by machines or left to make it on your own; surrounded by objects you care for or free of them; quiet or tuned in to the sound of others; warm or cool or even hot or cold.

Then go through days you'd like to spend, and ones you are likely to spend, noting in terms similar to those above how you would like to be in each room. Let's take, for example, the circumstances of a bath, for two very different people.

One would like to:

1. sweep into the bath
2. be undressed
3. seek shelter from view
4. but be with another
5. be indoors, but at the edge of a terrace
6. be in a large space
7. be in a bright and open space with afternoon sun
8. be served by a giant tub surrounded by warm walls of wood
9. be tuned in to the sounds of others
10. and be hot.

Another might prefer to:

1. squeeze into a tub
2. be undressed
3. seek shelter from view
4. be alone
5. be indoors
6. be in a small space
7. be in a sheltered space
8. be served by a bathtub free of objects
9. be quiet
10. and be hot.

This ten-point description should be recorded for each action of the day (where you'd like to be when you get up, go to the toilet, dress, cook breakfast, eat breakfast, wash the dog, fix the lawn mower, have a glass of sherry, entertain a friend, forget lunch, snooze, undress, sunbathe, bathe, fix dinner, welcome friends, mix drinks, relax on the terrace, eat dinner, talk to the friends by the fire, bid them good-night, leave the dishes, go to bed). It should be repeated to describe the actions of each adult member of the family. Then it will be helpful to make similar lists for the children in the family, for guests, service people, and pets. (We shall shortly note some special circumstances for some of these groups.) Next the lists must be added together, the redundancies removed, and the conflicts adjusted. You and your spouse, for instance, don't need separate fireplaces to sit in front of together; but if you and your beloved want to sleep together, one in a large sunny room and the other in a dark cozy room, there will have to be a compromise or someone's clear-cut victory.

We keep this choreography abstract because we want to avoid casting your actions too quickly into stereotypes—for instance, a living room, which would almost inevitably be compared with Mrs. Jones's altogether admirable living room nearby, or a family room which would be okay because family rooms are in, or a morning room which would not be okay because morning rooms are out. The abstraction is also a help, we reason, because some of the spaces in the typical suburban house are neither pleasant nor useful, and it would be helpful to bypass them altogether, to save money for spaces which might be inhabited with more pleasure.

All the lists you will have made will not give you enough information to determine a single solution for your house. But you should, with your lists and their combination, be able to judge the number of separate rooms you need, and what they might be

like. Then you can decide on the machine domains you need, and organize them as we have described, subjecting them to the test of the lists, amending the scheme (or discarding it, and developing another) until you have something that works. Keep trying. It is meant to be enjoyable, and as one of Le Corbusier's last books notes in its title, "Creation is a patient search."

Children

The children in your family need special lists made for them (or by them, if they are old enough). Children, remember, start out life smaller than adults, in a far smaller world, limited at first to their cribs, then expanding as their mobility increases. Experiences of space and light and motion and the opportunity for things to happen are all new in their lives. Teachers of children in slum areas note that environmental deprivation, the absence of experiences with the world around them, is as crippling a limitation as the lack of food and formal education. That this sensual deprivation is not limited to childhood or to poverty can be attested to by adults who frequent Holiday Inns. But the rewards for giving children the chance to open up their senses should be evident.

It is worth adding, too, that many children grow big before they grow well coordinated, and asking them to mince around in small spaces hemmed in by delicate objects may just be unreasonable. It is also true that childhood is a period of rapid change, and it doesn't do to plan too precisely for the requirements of a nine-year-old in a house he may not move into until he is ten.

Invited guests

Still other choreographies are required for each category of invited guests (your children's, or your own, for play or drinks or

3. A Japanese teahouse in Kyoto

4. Library, Danforth house, Madison, New Jersey, ca. 1880

bridge or dinner or a political meeting). It is striking, as people describe their requirements to their architects, what high priority they generally put on how they entertain —however infrequent those social occasions are: "Just two or three couples for dinner," or "Sixty for an occasional cocktail party." What it amounts to, of course, is that an important function of the house is *display* of yourselves, and it is generally the invited guests to whom the display is being made. As you chart the movements of your guests in the ten-part choreography, consider how they move, what they see (and what you hide from them), what they do, and how you want them to react to your display.

The Japanese tea ceremony was a celebrated instance of a highly ritualized development of the relation between host and guest, controlled in time and space from entry through a garden over carefully placed stepping stones to a pavilion from which all undesired clues had been banished (3) so the display could be focused on behavior, and on a few accessories of great worth. Rooms in the Victorian house (4) served similarly as a stage for display and for ritualized behavior, with a rather larger number of demonstrable objects used to tip the guests off to one's status and concerns.

In our own deritualized lives, the clues in the living room display may seem like— and they in fact may be, consciously or unconsciously—false, store-bought for uncertain purpose, as impersonal as the furniture in the last motel room you stayed in. If you mean to keep your guests at arm's length, this resolutely unrevealing anonymity may have real appeal. If you want to display your concerns more particularly, but on a stage apart from your family's lives, then, of course, if you can afford the space, you have that option. But the setting should be

complete, because if, for instance, your guests seek the toilet, you might be embarrassed to let them backstage. On the other hand you may want the life you live and the life you share with your guests to merge. In this way you can show them what you cherish and let their own patterns coincide with yours, maybe even when you cook or when you bathe. One of the chief issues as you choreograph your guests' patterns is how closely they really do coincide with your own. How open with them do you want to be? How open with your possessions and your own patterns of life?

Service people
With service people, if you ever have any, as with guests, an important issue is the intimacy, the congruence, of their movements with your own. Old houses often had back stairs to provide a circulation route for the servants. Also the routes of food and garbage, of dishes, of cloth, and of paper wastes which used to be presided over by servants were kept separate from the owner's paths. This may be why these routes still receive such scant attention. Try the ten-point choreography on your service people, and see if it modifies the patterns of your house.

The uninvited
A rather special group, to which you need not apply the whole ten-point test, is the uninvited; the burglars and marauders and vandals. The main issue here is how extensively you want to guard against them. The available devices include walls, locks, bars, and electrified systems which either ring a bell or phone the police or both when an intruder (or anyone else) forces a window or enters an area rendered sensitive. The price you pay is in money (several hundred dollars for a complete system) and in

265

nuisance (most acutely experienced when you inadvertently set off the alarm yourself). The payoff, of course, is a sense of security. Other warning devices, to detect fire or smoke or a malfunctioning furnace or power supply, may in some situations seem more to the point than protection against burglars. And if you are primarily worried about your possessions, adequate insurance may provide more security than any system of sirens or bells.

Pets

One last special group to be choreographed is your pets: do you have dogs, cats, horses, rabbits, mice, goats, or other animals about the house? Will you limit their paths with fences or cages or pens or leashes or screen doors? Or can they be trained so that physical restraints become unnecessary? Where will their paths cross the paths of food and dishes? Where will their waste join the path of waste, water-borne or otherwise? When will their paths coincide with those of family members? How will they be sheltered from the elements?

Images

When you have charted all the paths of water, air, paper, food, dishes and other cooking utensils, clothing and linen, electricity, dirt, cars, and other objects, then have choreographed the paths of adults, chil-dren, guests, service people, pets and the uninvited, and have sought the patterns in the intersections of all of them, you are left with the task of overlaying on all this the cast of your dreams. Then you can make a house which not only works but is in the mood you want it to be. This is to say not only that the rooms and machine domains are the right ones for you and at the right places, but that they feed your fantasies as well and make you feel at home (or however you want to feel).

Thus complete is the method we proffer for making a house you can care for: chart the paths of the things that go through your house, and of the people who will live in it; decide how many rooms and machine domains will accommodate all those, then squeeze and combine and pare until the place seems about as big as you can afford. Try the ways the rooms can fit together (there aren't very many), the ways they relate to the machine domains, and the way the whole fits the site; then when your try doesn't seem quite right, try again, not forgetting to honor your own images. Finally, it should feel right, able to receive you and to feed your enthusiasms. If when you have done all this you feel unsure about your capacity to realize your scheme in technical terms, seek someone with the expertise to help you—but don't let him stifle your dreams.

Inhabiting

Inhabiting

The prospects for building single houses are, of course, diminishing. Land which can be afforded for a single house tends now to be far from any recognizable communal center —on the fringes of previous suburbs or in once remote areas now available to interstate highway weekends.

The house, still the center of its owner's existence, thus unfortunately moves toward independence of its neighbors. It may share with them an imaginary freedom of stylistic choice, or instead may be submitted to some hoked-up stylistic constraints. But in either case there is seldom the genuine community of assent and common understanding that makes for a larger sense of place.

If lots are sold individually, it is usually to people too diverse in their background and style of life to engender much common action. More frequently of late, whole segments of landscape are developed speculatively, subjected to a particularly devastating mix of indifference, haste, and the compulsively bland imagery that accompanies low-risk real estate marketing. In this latter case, the buildings are built with no real inhabitants in mind and no point of view at all.

In frustration with, or disregard for, the difficulties of forging a sensible common order, the building industry has pretended a problem didn't exist, and many Americans (ourselves and most of our clients included) have sought out places where the world that each can comfortably care for is circumscribed by the boundaries of a building lot and the network of auto tracks that reach out from it. Each of us becomes nearly solipsistic—acting as though the world were entirely of his own making, inhabited only by those he knows, and animated by processes that each can command. This is a delusion. It is the delusion that is undoing the Sea Ranch, where those who would not make the imaginative effort required to share an environment already there have diminished its promise for others.

The disintegration of accord that can be recognized at the Sea Ranch is of course only an obvious example of a general phenomenon of contemporary culture. The American landscape is littered with the shards of successive environmental dreams. Our own dream, as architects, is of a built environment so richly configured that it can easily be claimed by the imagination, with recognizable places that can serve as bench marks and identification points. Our dream is of places to live in, endowed with a structure that can be used to make sense of, but not to restrict, the circumstances of daily life—not so much to mold the circumstances as to trace them.

In towns or large-scale developments, successive demarcations of space from street to sidewalk, to lawn, to stoop, to indoors or from path to gate, under shelter to courtyard, stairs, and entry door, all serve as guides to psychic orientation much as contours on a surveyor's map help us to visualize and understand landscapes that otherwise escape our grasp.

There are many elements that can contribute to this structuring, most of them presently neglected. The fundamental principle is that in places where people live all space should seem to belong to someone or something; space either should seem to be inhabited, as if it belonged to or could be claimed by particular groups of people, or should be understandable as part of a coherent larger order, such as the natural landscape or the traditional fabric of the town or a system of altogether new urban spaces.

The Sea Ranch, for instance, was based on the premise that a new community could be developed that would build upon the inherent qualities of the site without significantly detracting from its natural splendor. Each building was to be keenly tuned to its immediate surroundings and to be shaped as a part of the larger landscape. It now appears that this expectation required more attentiveness than most owners and architects could muster and asked too little in the way of building an assertive new settlement with its own landmarks. At the tree line, as we have noted, where fields meet forest or hedgerow, houses can discreetly occupy the edge, and generally the siting works. But in the meadows and on the bare hillsides themselves the balance has been lost—the sweep of the landscape is sullied by houses that have not found their place in any order, and that subtract rather than add to the whole.

Now that the close responsiveness to climate and site that was originally envisioned at the Sea Ranch has not been sustained, it is apparent that a clearer and less delicate imagery would have been in order. Having failed to preserve the order that was there, one would perhaps have done better to establish a compact and coherent settlement with its own complementary sense of place, as focused and as memorable as, for instance, Oak Bluffs is.

Establishing the larger order is difficult because it must be one that has some basis in communal assent. Oak Bluffs was initially a religious community; it has been sustained because so many units were built together. It now has the coherence of a tradition that particularly suits the conditions of a summer place. Santa Barbara was credible because the community's leaders shared an interest in an imagined heritage. Edgartown has a continuing building tradition, and its grid was a useful organizing geometry that has identifiable scale because it is surrounded by open country and because sectors of the grid have developed their own peculiarities. In each of these cases the imposed tradition allows particular interpretation, and these places are filled with the distortions and quirks that indicate the presence of real people making real choices. The outline is filled in, inhabited. The larger order works because it is clear that specific interests can be accommodated within it.

A difficulty that plagues larger-scale siting is that most of the images of large domestic buildings in our traditions are based on feudal or royal precedents. The formal hierarchy that we admire in these was supported by a social hierarchy possibly oppressive and at least anachronous. It may be that one of the attractions of barns is that they are buildings which claim the landscape without the immediate connotation of some commanding social presence (although we suspect that a close examination of ranching might belie this).

The existence of large-scale ordering of the environment is not in itself oppressive. It becomes so only when the formal structuring is so literally associated with use that it inhibits free-ranging improvisation and interpretation—when it controls rather than stimulates choice.

To our eyes the types of order that are least credible are those which sacrifice individual response to mindless repetition and stereotype. Indeed, the conceptual tools that have been developed for working with multiple housing are for the most part abused. Primitive devices of repetition and regulation have dominated the planning and building processes and removed the locus of decision making from the actual site to city hall or corporate headquarters. Rather than being informed by personal dreams and actions, development becomes governed by the conveniences of abstraction. The most prevalent tyrannies are ones of undiscriminating stupidity: buildings arbitrarily aligned by the T-square, the public space devoured by vast, minimum-standard roads and the entire structure of open space and enclosure determined by inflexible setback regulations. For instance, the space that is abandoned to setbacks belongs to the world of numbers. It does not reflect any evolving communal order or any personally shared decisions. Neither does it reestablish the natural order. Generally it is waste. The prevalence in suburbia of abstractly derived and slavishly

maintained lawns and side yards accounts for much of the atmosphere of bland indifference that is often conveyed by houses across our country.

If the places where we live are to reflect the act of living, they must be rooted in the present—in the actualities of sites and families. All space, we have said, should belong to something tangible, like a grove or a brook, an active street or a memorable and evocative form, or it should belong to someone. Space that is defined only by prohibitions on its use cannot belong to a living, inhabited world.

To seem inhabited, a place must show evidence that there are people about. There are a number of well-tried and traditional ways to people space. Among them, of course, there are all the symbolic forms of inhabitation. Life-size figure sculpture is the most literal, if infrequently used. The contemporary sculptor George Segal has made full-size, prosaic plaster figures that sit in fashionable drawing rooms. The effect is unsettling. More humorous is the vinyl cowboy who leans against the living room wall in the house of an architect friend of ours in England. A more familiar figure is Michelangelo's David which manages, with carefully outsized proportions, to inhabit the whole of the Piazza della Signoria in Florence and to help us belong there as well. (1)

Miniature figures are more common, to be found in one form or another in almost every living room. When used with deliberate fancy, as in the wall paintings of Pompeian villas, or the Moore house in New Haven, they can crowd a house with imaginary inhabitants and help to make one place imaginable as many.

More frequently, symbolic inhabitation takes the form of building shapes that are so closely related to human size that they

1. Monumental statues in the Piazza della Signoria, *Florence*

serve as proxy for the presence of people. Doors are the most ubiquitous of these, so common that they need special attention if they are to carry the connotation that someone might appear in them at any moment. Pediments, stoops, and embellished frames all aid this purpose. Windows, too, properly sized, can evoke human presence, especially when they are bay windows or when they open to a balcony. Familiar forms, when they bring to mind the presence of people, can dominate the exteriors of houses so that the mind's eye can practice dwelling there.

A second way that space becomes peopled is through evidence of the acts of attention that go into building and maintaining it. Houses that are built so clearly that you can trace the acts of building seem peopled as vigorously as those that carry more literal symbolism. The evidence of care in tending a place, as in gardens, and shiny doorknobs, is particularly evocative. It makes evident the human energy that brings a house to life.

Another way to make a place seem fully inhabited is to give emphasis to those parts of a building that are formed to the shapes and capacities of the body. Stairs are the most common example; they are a direct translation of the body's actions, and their slope calls out visual messages of movement and inhabitation. They also directly influence the acts of those who use them, and they may be shaped to call our attention to the people who walk over and around them.

Finally, there are the signs of occupancy: curtains drawn, windows open, tricycles, lawn chairs, automobiles being repaired—the telltale evidence of daily life. These automatic indications of inhabitation are often problematic. Architects and local gossips often spend much energy in suppressing them, for fear that they might show indifference and disregard for prevailing norms. When the common environment is treated as waste space, such telltale evidence is indeed negative, but the fault may often be in the structure of a place, which may not provide enough sheltered space for personal inhabitation of the common realm. Ledges, walls, and pergolas that lay partial claim to the common space of a street can also shelter more communicative signs of occupancy. Collections of special plants or even objects may be displayed there—totems staked out against submersion in the commonplace.

The common space in a housing group can also bring attention more directly to the people who are using it and set the stage for common endeavor. To do this effectively, the general scene may be broken into identifiable groupings, "rooms" in the landscape made to accommodate human use and scaled to be stages for the size groups that will inhabit them.

There can also be, in any common environment, space that is contestable, that can be temporarily claimed by passersby as a place to pause and talk, appropriated by a party that spills over the boundaries of its private space, or seized as their turf by the assembled children of the neighborhood. The American front yard usually is contestable in this way, but characteristically it is too empty to provide much incentive for inhabitation. Communal activity needs some type of impetus.

The most effective bonds between people are temporal. Festivities and special events, even daily rituals, bring people together in a shared structure of time that asserts community. Places that emphasize these common events can enhance the sense of inhabitation—a parking area shared by several houses that brings commuters together on their way to and from work, porches to spill out onto in the spring, or a small common for building snow forts and walking the dog.

Frederick Law Olmsted wrote in the early part of this century that there are three elements necessary to satisfactory places of residence: good neighbors, the institutions that good neighbors are likely to provide, and "good outgoings." The places that we go out into if they show personal signs of inhabitation can nurture our understanding and feed our enthusiasm.

With this we state our fundamental belief that it is unlikely that the whole environment will improve until houses are better built and their place better understood.

Houses, whether built singly or in multiples, can serve as centers for grasping the world and investing it with care and attention. We each need a place to store the trappings of our inner selves. But the conditions of our lives make it perilous for our concern to be closeted in private chambers and surrounded by acres of indifference.

The interdependent society that we live in can be reflected in places that are fully inhabited, where the spaces that are communally used are as various and as richly invested with personal care as the private places in which we dwell. This will not come about by the subtraction of effort. Those who seek to diminish personal involvement in buildings can only, in the long run, bring disaster on us.

What we must create is an environment that carries evidence of choice. We need an environment that we can comprehend in the way that we comprehend houses—as places that have been made by and for people, where the processes of systematic ordering and exchange that underlie our civilization are included within our grasp, bent to clear human purpose. We need places where people can exercise their wills and enjoy the willfulness of others within a pattern of accord that is physically rooted to the place —more enduring than, but enlivened by the transient interests of those who each day can give it new life and point.

Index